The Wuffings

Kevin Crossley-Holland is a poet, broadcaster and interpreter of the northern world. He is the author of new versions of *The Norse Myths* and translator of *Beowulf* and *The Exeter Book Riddles*, while his many books for children include *British Folk Tales* and the Carnegie Medal-winning *Storm*. His books of poetry include *New and Selected Poems 1965-90* and, most recently, *Poems From East Anglia*. He has collaborated with a number of composers, including Nicola LeFanu, with whom he has written two operas: *The Green Children* and *The Wildman*, which was given its première at the Aldeburgh Festival in 1995. He is a Fellow of the Royal Society of Literature.

Ivan Cutting is a playwright and theatre director. Born in 1953, he studied at Canterbury and Bristol before returning to his native Suffolk in 1981 to help start Eastern Angles. He has been Artistic Director since 1985 and has directed most of the company's work as well as devising and writing many of the plays. His most recent plays have been *Inheritance, Fields, The Pirates of Pin Mill, The Reaper's Year* and *Days of Plenty*. *The Reaper's Year* has been commissioned for transmission on BBC Radio 4. Married with one son, he lives in Harleston, Norfolk.

THE WUFFINGS

by

Kevin Crossley-Holland

&

Ivan Cutting

RUNETREE PRESS

LONDON

1999

© 1997, 1999 Kevin Crossley-Holland & Ivan Cutting

All rights reserved

Kevin Crossley-Holland and Ivan Cutting are hereby identified as authors of this work in accordance with Section 77 of the Copyright, Designs and Patents Act 1988.

All rights whatsoever in this work are strictly reserved. Application for permission for any use whatsoever, including performance rights, must be made in advance, prior to any such proposed use, to Eastern Angles Theatre Co. Ltd., Sir John Mills Theatre, Gatacre Road, Ipswich, IP1 2LQ.

This book is sold subject to the condition that it shall not, by way of trade or otherwise, be lent, resold, hired out or otherwise circulated without the publisher's prior consent in any form of binding or cover other than that in which it is published and without a similar condition including this condition being imposed on the subsequent purchaser.

Published by
Runetree Press
PO Box 1035
London, W2 6ZX

ISBN
1 898577 07 2

Printed and bound by
The Book Factory, 35–7 Queensland Road
London, N7 7AH

Typeset from the authors' disc by
Shaun Tyas
(Paul Watkins Publishing)
18 Adelaide Street
Stamford, PE9 2EN.

CONTENTS

Acknowledgements	vi
The Historical Background, *Ivan Cutting*	vii
A Personal Perspective, *Kevin Crossley-Holland*	xiii
Principal Characters	xvi
Other Characters	xvii
First Performance and Cast	xviii
THE WUFFINGS	1
Production Notes	120
Recommended Reading	123
Chronology	124
Glossary	125

ACKNOWLEDGEMENTS

The photographs are courtesy of Eastern Angles Theatre Company.

The photography is by Mike Kwasniak
(160 Sidegate Lane, Ipswich, IP4 4JF; tel: 01473–719002).

Translations into Welsh are by Eilian Wyn.

THE HISTORICAL BACKGROUND

In 1939, an amateur Suffolk archaeologist made a discovery which was to change the way English history is written. Excavations made at the site at Sutton Hoo, near Woodbridge in Suffolk, revealed the remains of a 90-foot ship which had lain in the ground undisturbed for 1300 years. The ship was all the more remarkable for the richness of the treasure found inside it: beautifully ornate gold jewellery and artefacts, some from Byzantium and beyond, a huge shield and other weapons, clothes and pots, and all the domestic goods to allow a pagan warrior make the last journey of all. This hoard showed off the Anglo-Saxons as a people with connections right across Europe, and as a civilisation that straddled a crucial period of change during which tribal chiefs developed into kings and pagan became Christian. Indeed the pagan burial itself offered up a beautiful pair of baptismal spoons marked *Saulos* and *Paulos*.

Although there was no immediate sign of a body, that ship is now widely assumed to be the last resting place of Raedwald, warrior king of the Wuffings, who were the royal house of the East Angles. And this majestic ship burial, dated around 625 AD, is now seen as a final pagan firework, a political act of defiance asserting the northern heritage of the Angles in the face of the growing tide of Christianity that was sweeping across the island of Britain.

This all seemed ideal and remarkably uncharted territory for the theatre. The more answers the archaeologists and researchers suggested, the more urgent became the truly human questions of why, how, and under whose direction? As I listened to someone like Martin Carver, current director of the Sutton Hoo Research Trust, in his off-the-cuff lectures referring to debates about concepts of kingship as 'arguments carried on in the language of ship burials', or proposing a growing sense of two cultures where the pagan meant chieftains, oral culture, runic imagery, bullion balances and burials, while the Christian meant kings, literacy, taxes, coins and monuments, I grew increasingly impatient to create a play about these people.

In 1991 I approached Kevin Crossley-Holland, whose poems, translations and stories I already admired, to talk about creating such a play. He was then teaching in America but his response was immediate, that he had to be involved and couldn't wait to get going. Although the timing was difficult for him, this was partly resolved by the length of time it took us to find the site and resources to mount the production. Nevertheless Kevin and I used the time to research, discuss and compare notes until in 1996 we sat down to construct a scenario. But where to begin?

The Dark Ages are not called dark for nothing. Sources are limited and the known facts are few. We started with Bede, who tells us that after

THE WUFFINGS

the Romans left, various peoples, Angles, Saxons and Jutes, from an area around what we know as north Germany and southern Denmark, arrived on the eastern shores of Britain. It seems to have been the Angles by and large who occupied the land from the Wash to the Stour, which is why the area became known as East Anglia. Perhaps one group or family was bigger, cleverer, better fed, stronger or merely attested to their own royalty, we don't know; but when they claimed ascendancy others believed them or obeyed them, and that was enough. They called themselves the Wuffings (the word means *Little Wolves*) and, like all the leading Anglo-Saxon royal families, traced their genealogy back to the god Woden. Seven names follow that of Woden before we reach Wuffa himself. We know nothing else about them until the arrival of Raedwald, except that their palace was at Rendlesham, less than five miles from Sutton Hoo.

Then it hots up. In 597 AD the Augustinian mission had arrived in England. It was welcomed by the southern High-King, Ethelbert of Kent, under the influence of his Christian wife, Bertha. Bede records:

> Raedwald ... received Christian Baptism in Kent, but to no good purpose; for on return home, his wife and certain perverse advisers persuaded him to apostasize from the true Faith... He tried to serve both Christ and the ancient Gods.[1]

Here was our central drama, a man who was trying to balance two ambitions, worship at two altars. All this was clearly for reasons of political expediency since some twelve years later, during which there has been no mention of him, Bede describes Raedwald as achieving his goal, even if his acknowledgement is somewhat grudging:

> Ethelbert was the third English king to become High-King of all the provinces south of the river Humber, but he was the first to enter the kingdom of heaven... The fourth [to hold such overlordship] was Raedwald, king of the East Angles, who during the lifetime of Ethelbert was winning pre-eminence for his own people.[2]

Notice that Raedwald is not expected in heaven. Apart from some further scandal from The Anglo-Saxon Chronicle, amid which Raedwald becomes High-King...

> 616 In this year Ethelbert, King of Kent, passed away: he reigned fifty six years. After him his son Edbald succeeded to the kingdom. He abandoned Christianity, having his father's widow to wife.[3]

---

[1] *A History of the English Church and People*, translated by Leo Sherley-Price, Penguin Books, 1955.
[2] *ibid.*
[3] *The Anglo-Saxon Chronicle*, translated and edited by G. H.

THE HISTORICAL BACKGROUND

...there is no more about Raedwald until the following year, his *annus mirabilis* according to the Chronicle:

> 617 In this year Athelfrith, king of Northumbria, was slain by Raedwald, king of East Anglia, and Edwin, son of Aelle, succeeded to the kingdom.[4]

Even Bede salutes this act of supreme military daring, which effectively made Raedwald king now of all land north and south of the Humber. It is the high point of his reign. But then, nothing. Apart from a Bede story of how Edwin came to be supported by the Anglian king, Raedwald peters out. The rest, as they say, is archaeology and guesswork. His sons are spoken of: Sigebert goes into Christian exile, only to return after Raedwald's (unreported) death; Ragenhere is killed at the battle with Athelfrith above; and Eorpwald, the youngest, succeeds to the throne and is baptised by Edwin. But Raedwald, he just vanishes, like the body in the acid sand of Sutton Hoo.

Yet Raedwald has enjoyed great success. If the date of his death is accurate, he rules his own kingdom for over twenty years, becomes High-King of southern Britain and nominally of northern Britain, suffers no defeats, enjoys good harvests, commissions the making of jewellery and treasure without rival in the whole of Europe, and sees his son on to the throne. Raedwald, apart from the battle with Athelfrith, is a prince of peace. Yet still Bede has little to say about him.

For us, there was a fundamental problem: how to get a man of dual belief to a decisive battle where he defeats a fellow pagan and to his own flamboyantly pagan burial. Unless Raedwald never really managed to make up his mind which side he saw himself on and the burial was a way of making him choose! What if Raedwald at and after his baptism believes that he can simply act the part of the Christian? Like the heroin addict he thinks he can handle it, but its power is all embracing and it eats into his soul. And it is this cancer of indecision that eventually destroys him.

Kevin and I went back to Bede again. Writing some hundred years after Raedwald's lifetime, the Venerable Bede had his own agenda, which was to chart the glorious rise of Christianity on this island. In this enterprise Raedwald fell short. For Bede considered Raedwald and his wife to be pagan. Bede saved his good words for Edwin, the Northumbrian prince who he regarded as instrumental in furthering Christianity's great success. It is one of Edwin's court who comes up with the famous metaphor of the sparrow flying through the hall.

But looking back to Edwin's relationship with Raedwald we started to see an interesting conjunction, and just about the only bit of psychological detail about Raedwald in Bede. This crucial moment occurs when

---

Garmonsway, Dent, 1953.
[4] *The Anglo-Saxon Chronicle, ibid.*

THE WUFFINGS

Edwin, in exile from Northumbria and sought by Athelfrith, the Northumbrian King, is given refuge at Raedwald's court. Athelfrith sends men to offer Raedwald a bribe to murder Edwin. Finally, Raedwald accepts, until, as Bede recounts

> [the Queen] dissuaded [Raedwald], saying that it was unworthy in a great king to sell his best friend in the hour of need for gold, and worse still to sacrifice his royal honour, the most valuable of all possessions, for love of money.[5]

Raedwald's grubby policy of *realpolitik* blunders into the ancient gods' code of honour about guests. Importantly, Raedwald accedes to his Queen. Edwin, however, despite being warned of Raedwald's initial decision to kill him, refuses to leave, saying he would rather be killed by Raedwald than a hand less noble. Impressed by this loyalty Raedwald spins about and determines to help Edwin regain his throne.

> [Raedwald] raised a great army to make war on Athelfrith and allowing him no time to summon his full strength, encountered him with great preponderance of force and killed him.[6]

Bede's delight, one suspects, is with Athelfrith's death and the ascendancy of Edwin, but more interestingly Bede ascribes to Edwin a different version of this moment. He attributes the warning of Raedwald's treachery to a vision, a vision which had prophesied that Edwin would be a Christian king of Northumbria.

Suddenly this moment seemed to combine the two cultures vying for Raedwald's heart. Why such a turn around on Raedwald's part unless his mind was already turning this way and that? The next question had to be under which banner does Raedwald fight Athelfrith: Woden's anvil or Christ's cross? The lure of Christianity is strong. It offers legitimacy for his laws, an inheritance for one of his sons, and a sense of purpose over the doom-laden fate of the pagan. But the fates are Raedwald's birthright and fill his head at every instance. He has just bowed to their demands for hospitality.

Slowly the truth dawned that Raedwald couldn't answer this question either. So what if he went into battle under both banners, combining the cross and the anvil, which the symbols so graphically do? He ensures that everyone has something to fight for and no one has anything to fight against. Being blessed by good fortune so far, he is unable to see any God as angry with him.

The result is a stunning victory, but in the process Raedwald loses his son, Ragenhere. What if Ragenhere as second son had been more of his mother's son and therefore still pagan? What if we tied in Sigebert's desertion to a Christian monastery in Gaul with the same event? It was

[5] Bede, *ibid.*
[6] Bede, *ibid.*

THE HISTORICAL BACKGROUND

possible. Then Raedwald loses two sons in this episode, one for each God that he has supported. He goes to his death unable to choose between the two ways. After this battle we hear no more of Raedwald, no report of his death, nothing, except the defiant shout of the ship burial. So who organised it?

Of course, any play where the central character must die before the final act might seem to commit dramatic suicide, but rescue was at hand. Someone organises the funeral arrangements and it is usually the wife. Why should it be different in Anglo-Saxon times, especially as Bede had already given us some clue as to her nature? The fact that Raedwald's Queen, whom we called Edith, is twice mentioned by Bede in terms of the strength of her pagan influence over the king shows that she was clearly some lady. All she needed was a genuine belief in the fates and the world of wyrd to order such an extraordinary finale for Raedwald's body.

Wyrd means, quite simply, 'what will be'. When the Anglo-Saxons used it, they were referring to everything that would happen because it was fated to happen. In mythology, the weavers of this fixed future were three demi-goddesses known as Fate, Being and Necessity. They took their instructions from Woden and, sitting beneath the World Tree *Yggdrasill*, spun the lives of each and every human being. Later pagans who converted to Christianity reconciled their new faith with wyrd by formulating the idea that 'Fate moves in the mind of God'. But for the play it was important that Edith's vision had to be real in her mind's eye and in her faith.

This was our story and our characters then divided into three: those taken from Bede (and therefore historical), those invented by ourselves, and those representing the pagan world of wyrd.

The historical characters are like the guy ropes holding the play in shape: Raedwald; Edith; Ethelbert, the old king of Kent who acts as Raedwald's godfather; his wife, Bertha; Augustine, the great missionary who ensured the new Christian religion simply took over the temples and festivals of the old religion; Edwin, the canny future king of Northumbria who brokered Eorpwald's conversion to Christianity; and finally the sons, Sigebert, Ragenhere and Eorpwald, in whose separate fates Raedwald's future really lay. Although we relegated the elder two to a mere symbolic presence, Eorpwald was seen and played as child and adult, and through him the crucial link to Edwin was established.

The non-historical characters argued themselves into the play to show the key forces of the time acting on the story: Leof, the court poet, who may have shaped *Beowulf* before it was christianised into the poem we now know; Puch, the fundamentalist and Roman Christian priest who must have bullied the dark and fate-ridden Angles towards his new God; Bebbe who represented the more amenable Northumbrian Christianity that was defeated at Whitby; Wulfgar, the trader who crosses seas and borders with the nonchalance of a modern commercial traveller; Wistan, the lieutenant who eyes promotion and harbours rejection; and Nia and her daughter Tanwen, the Welsh-Britons who feel out of place with the increasingly sectarian politics of the east, and yearn for their countrymen in the west.

Finally, we included elements of the Scandinavian gods brought by the Angles to Britain: the Norns, or sisters of wyrd, who fight to retain control of Raedwald's heart and mind and surround all the action; and Woden himself, who intervenes in Edith's vision to remind her of her mortality. Above all, we tried to capture a sense of the wyrd in the everyday life of the pagan believers. We know the Christians win in the end, so we had to show the pagans were no pushover.

What we hope we have written is some kind of version of the events leading up to and surrounding that great ship burial at Sutton Hoo. It is not an accurate account – it can't be when historians are still arguing over the order of events – and it is not a museum style re-creation. It is an imaginative account and some will argue with that, but we do believe profoundly in the theatre's duty to explore beyond known facts and ask 'what if?'.

To make this possible and to help our story flow, we have condensed events – Edwin was in exile at Raedwald's court for 8 years before Raedwald threatened to kill him. We have simplified – the pagan counteraction after Ethelbert's death and expulsion of bishops during Edbald's reign in Kent was much more complex. We have invented meetings – who knows if Edwin and his new wife-to-be called in on their way back to Northumbria to be present at Raedwald's death? And we have created new explanations where the opportunity was tempting – such as the role of the stag emblem from the treasure and our interpretation of Edwin's vision. Finally, we have accelerated some things – if Eorpwald finally became Christian at the prompting of Edwin of Northumbria, what matters is not the timing but our understanding of it. However, I hope we have remained true to the fundamental truth of the age and of this episode in history.

Since that original discovery at Sutton Hoo there has been much archaeological excavation both in the region as a whole, and crucially at Sutton Hoo itself. There is not space here to list all the theories and discoveries, but just to register our indebtedness to all those whose ideas we have pillaged, simplified and generally kicked about on stage. The theatre is a fairly common thief in these instances.

At the back of this book, there are some production notes on staging, a glossary of the various gods, and a chronology. All it remains to me to say is that Sutton Hoo marks the end of an era and the funeral of a culture that many think still lingers in the East Anglian psyche and outlook on life.

Ivan Cutting

A PERSONAL PERSPECTIVE

Each year I make a pilgrimage. I come back to the same, small, salt-wind-scoured, round-towered Norfolk church. I come back to a square eleventh-century font carved out of a massive hunk of Barnack stone.

On three sides this font is a kind of stone calendar. Here is a carving of January swigging ale from a horn, and February toasting his toes by the fire. March turns the earth with a curved spade, and April is pruning a vine. When I grasp the rough stone, it begins to warm to my touch. May is holding a banner and 'beating the bounds' – that is to say, walking the parish boundaries. June is mowing with his scythe; and July is busy raking. August binds a sheaf of corn, September threshes with a flail, and October is pouring ale into a vat. November is slaughtering a pig, and to illustrate December, there are four men sitting side by side, eating and drinking.

So here past and present meet. This wonderful font, sitting in a precious place that hasn't been 'discovered' or promoted as part of the heritage industry, records and celebrates the way most English people spent their hours and days and lives for century after century.

The poet, very likely an East Anglian, who composed the great seventh-century epic poem *Beowulf*, tells us about a wonderful feasting-hall in which there are treasures and tapestries and 'many a fine sight for those with eyes for such things'. Britain itself is like this. The whole island, says novelist Peter Vansittart, is 'an old house packed with memories'. We have only to open our eyes to see signposts all around us, pointing back through fifty generations and more to the age of the Anglo-Saxons.

Think of our coinage! Although we've set aside shillings and florins and half-crowns, we do still have pounds and pence; a few of them! Some of us don't greatly mind whether or not we trade them for Euros; but others care very much, and one argument advanced for retaining pounds and pence is tradition. Well, the retentionists do have a point. Our pence originated in Anglo-Saxon England while our pounds derive from Roman times. The symbols £ and *lb.* both stand for *libra*, which is Latin for pound.

Another signpost is our legal system. British law has its origin, however distant, in the law codes laid out by Anglo-Saxon kings. The first of them was handed down by Aethelbert of Kent, the king who appears in the first scene of *The Wuffings*, in about 602 AD. During the seventh century, too, rulers of English kingdoms began to succeed to the throne by virtue of primogeniture as opposed to what Raedwald, in our play, calls 'tribal jostling'. The anointing of a successor and the ceremony of coronation with its Christian blessing: these procedures, too, were first enacted in Anglo-Saxon England. Indeed, *Zadok the Priest* has been sung, first in Latin and now in English, at every coronation since that of King Edgar in 973 AD.

Of course we should visit museums and marvel at the tangible legacy of the Anglo-Saxons: glorious and glowing manuscripts, gold-and-garnet jewellery, soaring stone crosses. Of course we should read their poetry, so proud, so shrewd, so full of longings, so humane, so lyrical, and so witty. But the point is that the Anglo-Saxons are not only to be found behind glass or on the page. Theirs is the culture that started to shape the very fabric of English society, the look of our land, and our language.

Our quite small island has been intensively worked by many successive generations, and most of us live in it cheek by jowl. In virtually every village and town, there are buildings dating from medieval to modern times, and many individual buildings combine the work of different generations and centuries. In literally hundreds of English villages and towns there are churches with Anglo-Saxon features – little triangular windows, pilaster strips running vertically up walls, or 'long and short work' (stones set alternately upright and horizontal at the quoins, where wall meets wall). Your parish may have two or three Anglo-Saxon hedge-rows and ditches. And the name of the place itself may well point to its origin.

Henry James understood all this when he wrote, after visiting England, 'You feel custom and tradition – another tone of things – pressing on you from every side ... Morally and physically, it is a denser air than ours'.

Signposts! Each time you or I use English words, half of them come from Anglo-Saxon. On the whole, it is the good, tough, sharp, quick words that come from this root. Birth, child, meat, fish, man, woman, love, lust, earth, sea, plough, axe, sword, ship, old, year, death: all the words that tell us about the stuff of life here on middle-earth come from Anglo-Saxon while the polysyllabic language we employ to describe the abstract and conceptual derives from Latin and Greek.

Ivan Cutting writes of the way in which there may still be Anglo-Saxon strains within us. Is it true to say there is a dogged, stubborn strain in your make up? Do you relish the idea that when the going gets tough, the tough get going? Are you a fatalist? Are you inclined not to sentimentality but to melancholy? Do you have a strong feeling for the sea? Or a passion for ritual? I don't know whether it is useful or even possible to point to typical or enduring English characteristics. But if your answer to any of these questions is yes, then you share at least one quality with our Anglo-Saxon ancestors.

So I stand by my font, scribbling these words in the fading light. It is the eve of the summer solstice and, somewhere nearby, the 'merry wanderer of the night' is waiting in the shadows. Magic's in the air – and so, too, are the seabirds! As they scream and wheel round this round tower,

A PERSONAL PERSPECTIVE

I remember words from the Anglo-Saxon poem *The Seafarer* so full of passion and hunger that they seem like a hymn to our human need and sense of wonder:

> My heart leaps within me,
> my mind roams with the waves
> over the whales' domain, it wanders far and wide
> across the face of the earth, returns again to me
> eager and unsatisfied.

Kevin Crossley-Holland

PRINCIPAL CHARACTERS

RAEDWALD	King of the East Angles, age 35–55.
EDITH	His wife, Queen of the East Angles, 34–54.
EORPWALD	Their youngest son, 0–20.
AUGUSTINE	Leader of the mission from Pope Gregory, 60.
PUCH	Missionary priest, later Bishop, 26–46.
ETHELBERT	King of Kent and High-King of Britain, 45–56.
BERTHA	His Frankish Queen, 38.
NIA	Edith's serving-woman (Welsh), 40
TANWEN	Nia's daughter, 9–29.
LEOF	Poet at Raedwald's court, 50–70.
WISTAN	Nephew of Raedwald, 17–37.
BEBBE	Northumbrian princess from Kent, 38–47.
WULFGAR	Trader and craftsman, 37–57.
EDWIN	Exiled prince of Northumbria, later King, 29–38.
FATE	First sister of Wyrd
BEING	Second sister of Wyrd — the THREE NORNS
NECESSITY	Third sister of Wyrd

OTHER CHARACTERS

MESSENGER	From the Kent court.
NORTHUMBRIANS	Two men from Aethelfrith's court.
WIFE & CHILD	Of Edwin.
ATHELBURH	Edwin's second wife.
BLACKSMITH	
WODEN	Old God.
ATHELFRITH	King of Northumbria

plus non-speaking PRIEST, ATTENDANTS OF BEBBE, WARRIORS.

By doubling AUGUSTINE–EDWIN, NIA–BEBBE, ETHELBERT– WULFGAR and BERTHA–YOUNG EORPWALD, and some minor doubling, *The Wuffings* is playable with a cast of 15.

The action of the play takes place as follows:

ACT 1	*c.*605AD, Kent and Rendlesham.
ACT 2	*c.*616AD, Rendlesham.
ACT 3	*c.*616AD, Rendlesham and the River Idle.
ACT 4	*c.*616 & 625AD, Rendlesham.
ACT 5	*c.*625AD, Rendlesham and Sutton Hoo.

FIRST PERFORMANCE AND CAST

The Wuffings was first performed at Notcutts Nurseries, Pettistree, near Woodbridge, Suffolk, on 10 July 1997 with the following cast:

Puch	Alastair Cording
Augustine	Guy Moore
Ethelbert	William Haden
Bertha	Katherine Oliver
Raedwald	Stephen Finegold
Edith	Carrie Thomas
Nia	Janet Jefferies
Wistan	John Lightbody
Wulfgar	William Haden
Fate	Xenia Horne
Being	Pat Whymark
Necessity	Brierley Arnell
Leof	Tom Marshall
Tanwen	Melanie Barker
Young Eorpwald	Katherine Oliver
Bebbe	Janet Jefferies
Messenger	Dickon Edwards
Edwin	Guy Moore
Wife of Edwin	Brierley Arnell
Northumbrian Soldiers	William Haden
	Dickon Edwards
Blacksmith	Alan Edwards
Eorpwald	Dickon Edwards
Ethelburh	Katherine Oliver
Woden	Alan Edwards
Musician (Harp)	Xenia Horne
Musician (Guitar)	Jon Goddard

Other parts played by members of the company.

Director	Ivan Cutting
Designer	Fred Meller
Musical director	Pat Whymark
Lighting designer	Geoff Spain
Assistant director	Ben Harrison
Sound designer	Tim Speight

Original music by Pat Whymark

This King Raedwald ... was son of Tyttla, and grandson of Wuffa, after whom all kings of the East Angles are called Wuffings.

>Bede

What we call Wyrd is really the work of God about which He is busy every day

>King Alfred the Great, c.888 AD.

ACT I

SCENE I-1

April, 605 AD. A beach in Kent. The sound of the sea. Clouds race across the sky.

Three WOMEN sit threading nets, tending a fire and washing clothes in a pool. Over them stands a tree. Occasionally they swop jobs, sing, play music...

In the distance the sound of simple plainchant. Buffeted by the wind, AUGUSTINE, with two pieces of smoked glass over his eyes and wearing a pallium, is carried on a litter by two PRIESTS, singing. The first priest, PUCH, scans the beach.

PUCH [*Irritated*] Where are they?

The other PRIEST continues singing.

PUCH Set him down!

Both stop singing and lower the litter. AUGUSTINE's voice continues solo.

PUCH How do we know he won't change his mind?

AUGUSTINE [*Stops*] A pagan's word is as good as anybody's.

PUCH [*Disgusted*] Tchuh!

AUGUSTINE He'll come.

ETHELBERT and BERTHA follow on. Bertha is overdressed for the occasion and trying to retain her dignity.

BERTHA Why did we have to walk all the way out here?

ETHELBERT You know Raedwald. His pride. If Jutes can walk into the sea, so can he.

THE WUFFINGS

BERTHA goes up to AUGUSTINE and kneels to kiss his hand. ETHELBERT follows, but more awkwardly.

BERTHA   Augustine!

AUGUSTINE   His holy Father's servant welcomes the King and Queen of Kent to their own shore!

ETHELBERT   Why isn't he here? The weather's getting worse.

AUGUSTINE   Eight years ago there was a king who made me wait on Thanet island. He refused to meet me until the sky was clear to be sure I worked no spells on him.

BERTHA   Don't embarrass him.

AUGUSTINE   At least his wife wasn't so superstitious.

ETHELBERT   Unlike Edith!

PUCH   Over here!

BERTHA   Edith's not coming too, is she?

ETHELBERT   She wouldn't miss this!

BERTHA   Poor Raedwald!

From an opposite direction, a young man, WISTAN, appears and hurries up to ETHELBERT.

WISTAN   My king knows you are waiting, sir. We berthed up the river rather than bring the boat in here on this beach.

PUCH   Up the river..?

ETHELBERT   Trust an Angle. Old habits die hard.

EDITH, visibly pregnant, follows on with her Welsh maid, NIA, and RAEDWALD, wrapped in a large blanket. RAEDWALD is in his early thirties, tall and built like a rock. EDITH and NIA are wary.

ETHELBERT   Raedwald! You didn't need to go this far.

ACT I

BERTHA   Edith! How well you look!

ETHELBERT   The water has got ice in it!

EDITH   Does it matter what bit of the beach we use?

BERTHA   I am so glad about this.

EDITH   He takes his duty to the High-King seriously.

AUGUSTINE   Get me up, somebody.

AUGUSTINE assumes command as PUCH helps him stand.

EDITH   Yes, let us get on with it.

AUGUSTINE   Do you, Raedwald, King of the Angles, renounce the devil and all his works?

PUCH raises the crucifix. NIA looks up.

EDITH   [*To NIA*] What is the matter?

NIA   There is a storm on the way.

RAEDWALD   I renounce them all.

EDITH   Can they spellbind us if the sky is covered by clouds?

NIA   No. But the sky looks angry.

AUGUSTINE   Except a man be born of water and of the spirit, he cannot enter the kingdom of God.

RAEDWALD looks to ETHELBERT for guidance. ETHELBERT doesn't know. PUCH gestures to RAEDWALD to wait.

AUGUSTINE   The Lord is my shepherd: so I will want nothing. He will feed me in green fields: and bring me to the banks of healing waters. [*PUCH motions RAEDWALD to go now.*] He will stir my spirit: and lead me along the paths of right doing.

THE WUFFINGS

RAEDWALD casts off the blanket and walks slowly into the sea, hands outstretched. The sound of the waves increases until, when RAEDWALD is fully immersed, the sound becomes interior bubbles as if inside his head. As those on shore fix their gaze on RAEDWALD, the three NORNS appear from the sea.

FATE   Listen!

BEING   Raedwald!

NECESSITY   Listen!

FATE   Remember wyrd – all that will be.

BEING   Remember what is.

NECESSITY   Remember what must be.

The NORNS encircle RAEDWALD.

NECESSITY   You must think of your sons.

FATE   Sigebert.

BEING   And Ragenhere.

NECESSITY   And the son to come.

RAEDWALD walks to them to hear their message.

NECESSITY   We feed the Tree of Life. We spin your days – the whole length of your life. We choose your death-day. Only we know why you will die.

                Who is it keeps order in the nine worlds? Who but Thunor with his hammer in his thundering chariot. Worship Thunor!

                Bravest of the brave: who placed his hand in the jaws of the wolf Fenrir? Worship Tiw!

                Great goddess of the seed and the fruit. Who stands beside each woman in her hour of labour? Worship Frigg!

ACT I

Merciful and white-browed: who is the wisest of us all? Worship Baldr!

Who is she, the green one, stolen by the Christians? Worship Eostre!

Who hung on the tree for nine long nights? His side pierced with a spear. Woden! He shrieked and he died, then he rose again. Woden is the Raider and the Helmeted One. He is One Eye, Master of Magic, the Terrible One. All these names are one name. Woden is Allfather. Worship Woden!

FATE   Worship the great gods.

BEING   The great gods watch over the royal house of the Wuffings.

NECESSITY   House of the Little Wolves.

As the NORNS sweep away, RAEDWALD emerges from the sea.

ETHELBERT   We thought you weren't coming up again.

EDITH   This is madness!

RAEDWALD is freezing cold, but he warns her off.

AUGUSTINE   Give me your hand. [*RAEDWALD extends his left hand.*]

AUGUSTINE   The other one! [*RAEDWALD offers right hand. AUGUSTINE looks for water.*] Water!

PUCH   But...!

AUGUSTINE   I must have water. I can't bless the whole sea.

PUCH pulls up skirts and takes container and tries to collect some water as waves break and swash around him. EDITH starts to giggle. BERTHA stares at her.

NIA   Why's he so scared of getting wet?

AUGUSTINE   [*To PUCH*] That'll be enough!

THE WUFFINGS

PUCH returns and gives the water to AUGUSTINE who mumbles a Latin blessing over it.

NIA   What's he doing now?

EDITH   I don't know. Some kind of blessing on the water.

NIA   But it's the water that blesses him.

EDITH   Their ways are topsy-turvy.

BERTHA   Ssshh.

AUGUSTINE   [*Gestures RAEDWALD forward*] I baptise thee in the Name of the Father, and of the Son, and of the Holy Ghost. Amen.

BERTHA   Praise be to God!

AUGUSTINE   Amen.

PUCH   You haven't forgotten the letter?

AUGUSTINE   No, Puch, no. [*Fumbles in his pocket and pulls out a letter, which he then hands to PUCH.*] Brother Puch thinks I'm in my grave already.

PUCH   To our most excellent son, Raedwald, most glorious King of the East Angles, from your father in Christ, Pope Gregory. [*Makes sure they realise how impressive this is.*] Almighty God raises good men to govern nations, so that through them He can reward all the people whom they rule. [*AUGUSTINE motions PUCH to get a move on.*] My illustrious son, work to spread the Christian faith among your subjects. Make their conversion your first concern. Raedwald, God will reward you in heaven if you proclaim His Name on earth; and here on earth we will praise your name from generation to generation.

PUCH nods to RAEDWALD that it is all over.

AUGUSTINE   That was easy, wasn't it.

AUGUSTINE fumbles in his sleeves.

'God will reward you in Heaven if you proclaim His Name on earth.'
Puch (Alastair Cording).

THE WUFFINGS

AUGUSTINE   Raedwald, my own small christening gift. These silver spoons. See, the craftsman has cut an inscription on each handle. Words!

RAEDWALD looks, but makes no pretence of being able to read. He nods his head.

AUGUSTINE   [*Reading*] Saul ... and Paul.

BERTHA   Saul, in the middle of his life, on his way to Damascus, heard the voice and saw the light, the light from heaven. And then that pagan, the great enemy of Christ, became the great friend of Christ, the blessed St Paul.

NIA   They look like pears with long stalks!

EDITH   You need a long handle when you sup with these people.

RAEDWALD tries to speak but is too cold.

ETHELBERT   We should get you warm, Raedwald. We can't have your funeral before mine – not if you're to be my successor. Bertha! Look after Edith.

AUGUSTINE   Can someone set me down!

WISTAN, ETHELBERT and RAEDWALD exit.

BERTHA   Edith! Do you know how the Word came to this island?

EDITH   Word? I know nothing about word.

PUCH   In the beginning was the Word, and the Word was with God, and the Word was God.

EDITH   You brought your word all this way to replace our wyrd?

BERTHA   Edith! This man sailed to this shore only eight years ago but already he has consecrated twelve bishops.

PUCH   Alleluia!

ACT I

BERTHA   He has ordained hundreds of priests. On the day of Christ's Mass last year, following Ethelbert, their King, ten thousand men ran into the sea.

EDITH   Anyone can run in.

PUCH   But in the name of hope not fear.

AUGUSTINE   Be baptised in Christ, Edith, like your husband. Feed the infant Christ in this country.

BERTHA   Feed your baby, Edith, the Christ in your own baby.

EDITH   Before he's even born?

AUGUSTINE   A son you think? Then feed the king in your son! The Son in your king.

BERTHA   We need your help, Edith.

Rumble of thunder.

EDITH   The weather, look! Storm clouds.

PUCH   [*Calls the PRIEST.*] Quickly! Over here!

BERTHA runs, PUCH and PRIEST take AUGUSTINE off.

NIA   Thunor's angry.

A lightning flash.

NIA   Look, his chariot wheels!

EDITH   The harvest! Come, Nia.

A violent lightning-and-thunder storm crashes around the space.

SCENE I–2

RAEDWALD   Aaaargh.

THE WUFFINGS

RAEDWALD runs on in thick skin rug, jumping up and down to get himself warm. WISTAN follows him, carrying the king's clothing.

RAEDWALD Now I know why men who go overboard give up so easily.

WISTAN Uncle, you showed them all! And staying under for that length of time!

RAEDWALD dries himself and puts on his regalia.

RAEDWALD Is Ethelbert coming?

WISTAN The High-King said he would give you a few moments to collect your thoughts. Will he offer you the succession now?

RAEDWALD If he doesn't, I'll want to know why not.

WISTAN Will I have to become a Christian?

RAEDWALD In time, perhaps. Let's wait and see.

ETHELBERT enters.

ETHELBERT Walking into winter water! Trust Raedwald to show us how it should be done!

RAEDWALD If ten thousand Jutes can run in, an Angle can walk in.

ETHELBERT It was a poke in the eye for Puch!

RAEDWALD Is it that Puch who will come home with us?

ETHELBERT I am afraid so. Augustine is no fool.

RAEDWALD Wistan, go and make sure we are ready to sail tomorrow morning. I am worried that Thunor's tricks ... [*an embarassed pause*] I mean the storm may have hurt our next crop.

WISTAN exits.

ACT I

ETHELBERT A good enough man.

RAEDWALD Nothing a battle would not put right. That or a woman! I promised his father I would raise him.

ETHELBERT He looks up to you like a son.

RAEDWALD Even more so when he serves the High-King.

ETHELBERT Your turn will come. I've got some years left in me yet. The reins of the sisters are still in my driving hand.

RAEDWALD Is there room for the sisters of wyrd in a Christian heart?

ETHELBERT For fifty years they wove my fate. I can't wipe that away.

RAEDWALD I knew it! [*They embrace.*] As the saltwater covered my head I heard them calling me.

ETHELBERT I know that feeling. You have to become deaf.

RAEDWALD Why have we got two ears then? To listen to this – to listen to that!

ETHELBERT Don't misunderstand me, Raedwald. If you want to be High-King after me, you have to convert your people. One little splash today is not enough.

Roll of thunder in the distance.

RAEDWALD But what does your new God give you?

ETHELBERT Authority to govern. I can make new laws in God's name. Power to change taxes.

RAEDWALD I have those things, they were handed down to me.

ETHELBERT But you need force to keep them. This new God gives recognition by law. Whoever knew whose side the old gods were on? But this Augustine, he comes to you!

RAEDWALD But the threat of Thunor's hammer ...

ETHELBERT Stop! Enough of this fencing with old shadows. Our God is Christian and his victory must be total.

'But what does your new God give you?'
Raedwald (Stephen Finegold).

ACT I

RAEDWALD   That is your true belief?

ETHELBERT   Belief? Who talks of belief? I am talking about my people and the future of this land. Within Christendom, our force, our power, our influence, will grow... and our sons will be kings.

SCENE I–3

Sunset. EDITH and NIA enter with a dish. They take a flame from the fire and set alight the contents. Thunder rumbles in the distance.

NIA   Thunor's wild and furious.

Nia (Janet Jefferies) and Edith (Carrie Thomas).

EDITH   Let us begin.

NIA sprinkles leaves on the dish to create smoke. They kneel before it, clap loudly three times and chant:

THE WUFFINGS

NIA/EDITH   Storm, storm, great storm!
              Rule mankind on middle earth.
              Settle quiet as the summer ocean.
              Storm, storm, great storm!

NIA pulls out a Thor's hammer, shaped like a Tau-cross, and stands it on its handle.

NIA   Son of earth.

EDITH   Son of earth! Father of the neighing wind! Thunor the striker!

NIA   Peace to the whetstone in your head.

EDITH   Peace to the wheels of your chariot. Give us fair winds and green showers, give us.....

NIA   I see a shape, I see a man-shape, striding the waves......

RAEDWALD walks in. He has come to Edith's room. He stares at them.

EDITH   Have you come to join us?

RAEDWALD   Not here!

EDITH   Why not?

RAEDWALD   We are the guests of Ethelbert and Bertha.

EDITH   Didn't you see the storm?

RAEDWALD   Nia, wait outside for your mistress.

EDITH   Stay, Nia. Keep the flame alive.

RAEDWALD   They agree to baptise me in the open air and you repay them with this...

EDITH   Repay? Repay? Is that the language of our prayers now? Our people could starve this autumn following that storm. Supping with that old man's spoons has spotted your nose.

ACT I

RAEDWALD   And would you undo all we came here for, for the sake of waiting one more day?

EDITH   He has offered you the succession?

RAEDWALD   On condition. [*RAEDWALD looks at NIA.*]

EDITH   Nia, you can start packing.

NIA goes. RAEDWALD takes a candle and joins EDITH.

RAEDWALD   Does it matter which flame lights our way? As long as a Wuffing can be king. And these Christians like kings, they like to know who is in charge!

EDITH   Because they like to give the orders themselves.

RAEDWALD   So you will be happy as Queen of the East Angles, when all this land is on offer.

EDITH   All of the land? Athelfrith might have something to say about that.

RAEDWALD   Athelfrith's far away in Northumbria. He's too busy worrying about the Scots up his arse.

EDITH   What do we have to do?

RAEDWALD   Take the priest home with us. The rat-faced one.

EDITH   That little shit!

RAEDWALD   We just add their altar – we set it beside ours.

EDITH   [*Smiles*] Think of the danger. They might breed.

RAEDWALD   My storm-goddess! All bristle and brightness.

RAEDWALD and EDITH kiss.

WISTAN   [*Off*] Wulfgar! Wulfgar! We must prepare to sail in the morning.

EDITH   Raedwald, High-King! I can almost taste it.

THE WUFFINGS

RAEDWALD   It's the salt from the sea.

EDITH and RAEDWALD kiss passionately.

SCENE 1–4

The NORNS sing as the boat is built and WULFGAR, WISTAN, NIA and others take their place. PUCH with kitbag weaves in and out of the portside business and nearly gets knocked over. Once the boat is built WULFGAR stands at the stern with his hand on the tiller. AUGUSTINE is helped on by BERTHA. PUCH waves.

PUCH   Right! What are my marching orders?

AUGUSTINE   Not too much marching, Puch. Tread softly. I want you to deal carefully with these people.

PUCH   Angles! I'm told they are like carthorses, and just as stubborn.

AUGUSTINE   Then you will be a match for each other. [*PUCH is not impressed. BERTHA laughs.*] Listen to me!

PUCH   Your grace..

AUGUSTINE   You must trust our Holy Father. The temples of the idols should on no account be destroyed, but cleansed with holy water. Let them make sacrifices as they have always done – but in the name of God.

PUCH   Trust me. I will do as you command, for the glory of God.

RAEDWALD and EDITH arrive to board the boat.

AUGUSTINE   I will send my missionaries after you.

BERTHA   God speed you a safe journey.

PUCH kisses AUGUSTINE's hand. NIA and WISTAN watch.

NIA   Now he kisses his ring. [*They laugh.*]

ACT I

RAEDWALD   Silence! [*He helps EDITH on.*] Prepare to leave, Wulfgar.

WULFGAR helps PUCH settle.

AUGUSTINE   You will find the Lord. [*RAEDWALD turns to listen.*] You are still Saul. Become Paul.

RAEDWALD   You talk like the three sisters of wyrd.

AUGUSTINE   Once you glimpse the light, what can you do but follow it?

RAEDWALD   [*Offers hand*] I doubt we will see each other again.

AUGUSTINE   Unless in heaven.

WULFGAR   Right!

The boat starts to move. PUCH leans out to AUGUSTINE.

PUCH   The helmsman says we never lose sight of land, 'If Aegir wills it'. Who is Aegir?

BERTHA   He's their God of the oceans.

AUGUSTINE   Neptune! You see, Puch? This is your challenge. When you sail in with new words, new ideas, do not threaten them or they'll go back to their old beliefs. Do not cut away their traditions. Do not ridicule them.

SCENE I–5

The boat is at sea and rolling. WULFGAR, a solid man, commands the ship from one end, with WISTAN by him. RAEDWALD, deep in thought, sits at the other with EDITH. PUCH, very sea-sick, is in the middle with NIA, who turns her palms to the sea for a rowing song.

>   Salt waters, holy waters,
>   We are your children –
>   Your sons and daughters!
>
>   Nine waves, nine mothers,

THE WUFFINGS

> Nine ringing waves of the sea:
> Guide us home, safely home
> From the bells of Canterbury.
>
> Salt waters, holy waters
> We are your children –
> Your sons and daughters!

As the song continues, time passes and the weather calms down. PUCH stays by the side, retching.

WULFGAR   Hasn't anyone got a riddle? That would quicken the way. [*No answer*] Well, what about this then? 'I saw a strange contraption, a seasoned traveller, grind against gravel and move away screaming...'

EDITH   A boat.

WULFGAR   You're too quick.

NIA   You're too slow.

WULFGAR   Most women don't complain. [*NIA giggles*]

NIA   I've got one. This will cheer us up:
I'm a strange creature, for I satisfy women...

WULFGAR   Very strange!

EDITH   Very rare!

NIA   Do you mind?
I'm a strange creature for I satisfy women,
I grow very tall, erect, in a bed,
I'm hairy underneath...

EDITH   Nia!

NIA   From time to time
A beautiful girl dares to hold me,
Grips my russet skin, robs me of my head
And puts me in the pantry! Her eye moistens.

EDITH   Well, we all know what that is! Puch?

ACT I

PUCH   Disgusting!

RAEDWALD   Shame on you, Nia!

NIA   But you don't know! Do you?

WULFGAR   I know.

NIA   You like to think so.

WISTAN   It's an onion.

NIA   I didn't think you were listening. Your turn.

WISTAN   I'm over the side and behind you
Yet here in the boat and before you.
I'm rainbow-coloured but clothed in black,
I'm inside out and on the rack?

WISTAN looks over to where PUCH is recovering from his latest heave. The others start to laugh.

WISTAN   [*Pukes*] Puch! [*PUCH smiles.*]

WULFGAR   He's still got some Christianity left in him!

PUCH   I heard a radiant ring, with no tongue,
Intercede for men, though it did
Not raise its voice or argue...

EDITH   A bell.

RAEDWALD   A bell has a tongue.

PUCH   This peaceful treasure pleaded for mankind:
'Heal me, save me, helper of souls.'

NIA   I don't get it.

EDITH   Well?

PUCH   A chalice. The cup from which we drink the blood of Christ.

THE WUFFINGS

EDITH That is disgusting!

PUCH Christ gave his blood on behalf of mankind.

NIA And what do we get out of this God of yours?

PUCH Your sins are cleansed.

NIA What, all of them? Does he know I'm Welsh?!

EDITH [*to RAEDWALD*] Why so quiet?

RAEDWALD The Christian God. We must give him time.

EDITH You're thinking too much. Trust Raedwald!

RAEDWALD But our sons, if they are to rule...

EDITH Stop gnawing the bone.

A crack of thunder.

NIA This storm-god is travelling around us! I worry for Tanwen when he brays like this.

WULFGAR Watch out everybody!

The boat lurches about.

RAEDWALD What's happening?

WULFGAR We're between the two sea-paths.

NIA Aegir's angry. Down on your knees!

WULFGAR pulls EDITH down. WISTAN follows.

EDITH Smile on us, Aegir.

NIA Soothe the waves, rein the tides, open the way to our home.

The boat is hit by a huge wave. RAEDWALD decides to join the rest.

ACT 1

WISTAN Nia!

RAEDWALD Great skyfather, help these wanderers.

NIA/EDITH Open the way! Open the way to our river.

Everyone gasps as the boat heaves once more. Then peace.

WULFGAR That's it, everyone. We're over the bar.

RAEDWALD The bar! Of course.

ALL [*Sing*] Nine waves, you nine mothers,
Nine singing waves of the sea:
Carry us home to Rendlesham
Where my own daughter waits for me.

RAEDWALD watches everyone relax. There is a sense of everyone having over-dramatised the situation.

ALL [*Sing*] Salt waters.

WULFGAR The tide's flowing our way.

ALL [*Sing*] Holy waters.

WULFGAR We'll drop anchor at Woden's bridge.

ALL [*Sing*] We are your children –

PUCH Where?

ALL [*Sing*] Your sons and daughters!

WULFGAR Woden's bridge, just under the Hoo.

WULFGAR There it is. Look! There it is everyone! The Hoo.

PUCH What is it?

NIA The Hoo.

WULFGAR Now I know I'm home.

THE NORNS sing as the travellers climb out of the boat and tie it up.

THE WUFFINGS

RAEDWALD   My father's crossing place, and my grandfather's crossing place, Wuffa himself. And Woden, our first father, Woden. All the fathers of our House of the Little Wolves.

EDITH   Speak to them!

RAEDWALD   Bone-ground! Spirit-leap! Home to the Hoo.

TANWEN and LEOF appear over the brow of the Hoo.

NIA   [*Points*] There she is! [*Waves*] Tanwen! White fire! [*TANWEN waves back.*] She's grown taller while I've been away!

EDITH   The sisters foresaw our safe return.

RAEDWALD   Then they foretell what I have done is right. It will preserve our land, our people, our dynasty, our sons. Where are they?

SIGEBERT and RAGENHERE appear with the NORNS

BEING   Son of Woden! Blood of Woden! Raedwald, blood of Woden's blood!

FATE   Your fate is to lie here.

BEING   You are King of the Wuffings, guardian of this bone-ground.

NECESSITY   You must honour them, the old ones who sailed here from Sweden. Remember Raedwald, remember.

FATE   Your sons, Raedwald – your little wolves. Will they be kings after you?

BEING   What could be and what must be: where do they meet?

NECESSITY   Honour them, Raedwald.

FATE   Those who died live in you.

NECESSITY   Look back to look forward.

ACT I

SCENE I-6

The great hall. Benches fill its length. A fire burns in a central pit around which NIA and TANWEN bustle preparing food. WULFGAR enters with his arms round WISTAN. Others sit around on benches. PUCH sits on his own.

NIA	How was the storm?
TANWEN	What storm?
NIA	You had no storm?
TANWEN	Just growls and rumbles away south.
WULFGAR	Food! I could eat a raven.
NIA	Hands off until we're ready.
WISTAN	I'm only just getting my stomach back. I thought we were all lost.
TANWEN	Did you call out for your mother?
WISTAN	No!
TANWEN	I bet you did!
WULFGAR	Those tides, they're sharp-tongued. I should have warned you.

They turn as LEOF enters. An older man, he clearly commands their respect.

WULFGAR	Leof, at the mouth of the river, is it still Aegir, or the river spirits?
LEOF	It's both, whispering to the three sisters who weave your fate, who know the day of your death.

PUCH stands and everyone watches him in silence.

PUCH	Is that what you believe?

THE WUFFINGS

LEOF   Believe? We don't believe. Wyrd is!

PUCH   And what *is* wyrd?

LEOF   Wyrd is our fate. Our lives are shaped by the web the sisters weave, everything that is, everything that will be.

PUCH   Then why should men do anything?

LEOF   There's many a man who has died because of his own carelessness. When he wasn't fated to die. Why should a man do anything? Because our dignity, our names, the fame that lives after us is in our own hands.

PUCH   So Raedwald will win fame for his wise choice of Christ?

LEOF   [*Laughs*] Does it look like it's the talking point?

PUCH   Well, I haven't finished yet.

LEOF   No. No, you haven't even begun.

WISTAN chases TANWEN round the fire.

NIA   Tanwen, stop fooling around and get the jug. A gwna fel mae rhywun yn dweud 'tha ti! [Welsh: *And do as you are told!*] Where are you off to next, Wulfgar?

WULFGAR   Sweden. [*To those sitting.*] And which one of you is coming with me?

RAEDWALD enters with EDITH and his sons, SIGEBERT and RAGENHERE. LEOF takes up a bowl, commanding silence.

LEOF   The king belongs in his hall.

EDITH offers the bowl to RAEDWALD, who drains it.

RAEDWALD   We are safely returned, just! The crop is unhurt and we pray for a good harvest. [*Looking at EDITH.*] In the fields and in this palace. If Nia is right and it is a third son after Sigebert and Ragenhere, he will be called Eorpwald. The future of the Wuffings is secured.

ACT I

> But this is a time of change also. You know or you have heard that I have taken the Christian God into my heart and I welcome his servant into our midst. The king's eldest son, Sigebert, will be taught first by Brother Puch.

EDITH   We haven't talked about this!

RAEDWALD   The journey told me. But first, Leof! Your story! A story of a hero! Our own kin, Beowulf.

LEOF takes centre stage and waits for attention.

LEOF   Grendel, the monster, loped down from the moors!

Everybody arms themselves with food from the table to make the sound effects to go with the story.

> He came to Heorot, hall of old Hrothgar.
> The door, bolted with iron bands,
> Burst open at a touch from his hands.

LEOF enacts the story, using warriors as his victims. They all laugh.

> Ugh! The fiend stepped in, and he grinned
> When he saw many men, a group of Geats,
> A knot of warriors, sleeping in the hall.
> For a start he grabbed the nearest man,
> A tasty Geat, and he greedily wrenched him,
> Bit into his body, drank the blood
> From his veins, and chewed huge pieces:
> His head, his heart, even his feet and hands.
> Yes, he swallowed the whole man,

LEOF now switches round the roles and becomes Beowulf, but grabs PUCH and turns him into Grendel.

> But then Grendel grabbed Beowulf.
> Beowulf sat up – he gripped the monster's hand.
> Grendel could feel his fingers cracking!
> Then all the Geats woke up!
> They all swung their sharp swords!
> The hall-room boomed, and clang
> And clatter shattered the night-silence.
> No good! No use! No war sword,

THE WUFFINGS

>   Not even the finest iron on earth,
>   Could so much as scratch evil Grendel.
>   The monster had woven a secret spell
>   Against each kind of battle-blade.
>   Now Beowulf gripped Grendel's right arm.
>   He held him in a vice and very slowly
>   He turned the monster's arm behind his back.

ALL   Down!

LEOF   The warriors shouted.

ALL   Down, Grendel!

LEOF   You dardledumdue!

ALL   You dardledumdue!

LEOF   Beowulf locked and twisted the monster's arm,
            He tore Grendel's shoulder. His sinews
            Sprang apart, his muscles burst!
            Grendel howled. Glory in battle
            Was given to Beowulf.

ALL   Beowulf!

LEOF   And Grendel? He sobbed as he loped off
            Over the moors; he made for his stinking lair,
            Leaving a path of shining life-blood.

PUCH is left in a heap, as if defeated.

WISTAN   Well? What do you think of our hero?

PUCH   In the beginning God gave us bright life and free will. He wishes to remind us of those gifts through the courage of such as Beowulf. He is a true warrior of Christ.

LEOF   No, Puch, no.

PUCH   A warrior of Christ in the fight against evil.

LEOF   No, Puch. Beowulf knew his wyrd, not your word.

Leof (Tom Marshall).

EDITH	No wonder your Christ was hung up beside thieves!

LEOF	Beowulf, he worshipped the gods and the gods smiled on him. During his life and up to his death-day.

PUCH watches as everyone lines up into the shape of a longboat and creates a dirge. Over the top of this sound the NORNS wail.

> A maiden intoned a dirge for Beowulf time after time,
> declared she lived in dread of days to come.
> Then the Geats built a barrow on the headland.
> They bequeathed the gleaming gold, treasure of men,
> to the earth, and there it still remains
> as useless to men as it was before.
> People will say that, of all kings on earth,
> He was the kindest, the most gentle,
> Most just to his people, most eager for fame.

ACT II

SCENE II–1

Rendlesham 616 AD. Bright sunlight fills the stage. TANWEN and WISTAN sit amongst stooks of corn. WULFGAR prepares a bed roll.

TANWEN   [*Sings*] Summer opens my door: he's dressed in green.
He says it's the season for long journeys.
Ah, the land of my mother.

LEOF   Eleven more harvests came and went, each of them abundant, each sending one man over the whale-road to buy beaver skins and walrus ivory, wax and birch bark, garnets, cowry shells ...

EDITH   Where are you off to now?

WULFGAR   Byzantium!   [*WULFGAR says his farewells.*]

LEOF   One grew tall [*WISTAN gets up.*]

And one grew up. [*WISTAN helps TANWEN up.*]

And then one and one grew apart. [*TANWEN haughtily walks away from WISTAN.*]

While one man waited.... [*RAEDWALD gazes into the distance.*]

EDITH   Ethelbert can't last forever. Can he?

TANWEN   Misted autumn shadows at my door,
She smells of corn and smoke. She smells of sunlight.
Ah, the land of my mother.

LEOF   One prospered [*PUCH takes a light from the fire and starts lighting candles on his altar.*]

As one grew more thoughtful. [*RAEDWALD watches PUCH*]

Wulfgar (William Haden) and Nia (Janet Jefferies).
'The sisters cut the cords of one whose life was ended.'

THE WUFFINGS

TANWEN   Bony winter barges in.
          Silver-black and howling round the hearth.
          Ah, the land of my mother.

EDITH   What news?

LEOF   And still one waited.

MESSENGER hurries in and up to EDITH.

MESSENGER Queen Bertha is ill.

RAEDWALD   How much longer will Ethelbert go on for?

LEOF   During that time a boy became a youth and then a man.

[*SIGEBERT is brought on.*]

PUCH   Is Sigebert ready for instruction?

RAEDWALD takes SIGEBERT over to PUCH.

LEOF   A child became a boy and then a youth. [*RAGENHERE is brought on.*]

WISTAN   Shall I teach Ragenhere to fight?

EDITH   No. Ragenhere learns with me.

LEOF   And a baby became a child and then a boy. [*YOUNG EORPWALD runs on to play.*]

EDITH   You can look after Eorpwald, Wistan.

TANWEN   Welcome whistling spring! Pale-skinned
           And so cold to the touch, but promising.
           Ah, the land of my mother.

LEOF   The sisters cut the cords of one whose life was ended.

A NORN covers NIA, who gets up and goes. EORPWALD and WISTAN take the blanket and give it to TANWEN.

LEOF   Still one waited and waited and waited.

ACT II

PUCH — And God said to Abraham, you must sacrifice your own son.

The MESSENGER arrives again.

MESSENGER — Queen Bertha has died.

PUCH — I am sorry.

RAEDWALD — So am I.

PUCH — Your Godmother did so much for her people.

RAEDWALD — Oh yes. Of course.

PUCH — After eleven years perhaps it is time for a further sign that you believe in the true God.

RAEDWALD — You have my eldest son. What more do you want?

PUCH — He makes his own choices now.

RAEDWALD — The new God has shown an open hand. Eleven good harvests and we are rich. All I need is the golden harvest of the High-King's crown. Even Athelfrith in the north will have to bow before me then.

PUCH — But many of your people still worship the old Gods. Your Queen makes sacrifices. Will Raedwald let his people be damned for ever?

RAEDWALD doesn't know.

PUCH — Find peace in the arms of Christ.

RAEDWALD — Thank you, brother Puch.

PUCH returns to setting up their altar. LEOF enters.

LEOF — More news from Kent. Our High-King has taken a second wife.

RAEDWALD — News comes fast from that quarter. But still not the news we wait for.

RAEDWALD goes. LEOF turns to TANWEN, who is washing plants, but she turns her back.

WISTAN [*Off, calling*] Eorpwald! Eorpwald!

EORPWALD tears in and hides behind TANWEN.

EORPWALD Don't tell Wistan I'm here.

WISTAN [*Off*] Eorpwald!

TANWEN [*Shouts*] He's not here!

WISTAN enters.

WISTAN Did you call?

TANWEN I was just telling you the boy's not here.

WISTAN reads her face, moves and catches EORPWALD.

EORPWALD How did you know where I was? [*EORPWALD runs off.*]

WISTAN He's meant to be following me.

TANWEN Why's he come over here then?

WISTAN You know he always had time for your mother. All her gibberish.

TANWEN Don't know what you mean.

WISTAN [*Mimics*] 'Don't know what you mean.' It's half sing-song, like all your language. I heard her once with Leof. Do you speak it?

TANWEN Might do.

WISTAN Tanwen!

TANWEN Does your wife know where you are?

TANWEN moves off to wash vegetables. WISTAN follows.

ACT II

WISTAN   Why doesn't anyone else speak that tongue of yours?

TANWEN   It's secret.

WISTAN   Leof says they all talk like that over the west way.

EORPWALD runs in with a bunch of wild flowers.

EORPWALD   Here you are, Tanwen. They're wild like you.

TANWEN   You carry them. You can see my hands are full.

EORPWALD   [*Turns to WISTAN*] Wistan, can't we go bird nesting?

WISTAN   Climbing! Chasing! Nesting! Later. [*He relents.*] Go and find me a stick then.

EORPWALD   I thought I was supposed to be following you. [*Thrusts flowers into WISTAN's hands and then rushes off.*] I'm going to be in the fleet that sails north and smashes Athelfrith.

WISTAN   Don't say I said that. [*Turning to TANWEN*] I get fed up with this baby-watching. I was wondering, Tanwen.

TANWEN   So was I!

WISTAN   Do you serve the queen like your mother used to?

TANWEN   Don't know what you mean.

WISTAN   She still has an altar to the old gods in the temple. People say the King worships there as well.

TANWEN   You know people.

WISTAN   I just want to know which way the corn's lying.

RAEDWALD appears.

TANWEN   Here comes your master. Ask him.

WISTAN thrusts flowers at TANWEN, who is so surprised she takes them.

RAEDWALD   Ever the ladies' man, Wistan.

WISTAN   Sir, I didn't pick them ...

RAEDWALD   Where's Eorpwald?

WISTAN   Er... climbing, I think.

RAEDWALD   Is this your idea of training? Never mind, Wistan. King Ethelbert.

WISTAN   Yes, sir.

RAEDWALD   He remembers you. He remembers me saying you could do with a sword and a woman.

WISTAN   I was only young then, sir.

RAEDWALD   Yes. So he's sending you a wife.

WISTAN   I have a wife.

RAEDWALD   Well now you've got another one.

WISTAN   I don't want another one.

RAEDWALD   And I don't want to offend Ethelbert.

WISTAN   Are you mocking me?

RAEDWALD   Wistan, we wait daily for the High-King's death so I may assume that title. That's what you want as well, isn't it?

WISTAN   I'd rather have the sword.

RAEDWALD   Would you?

WISTAN   Athelfrith and his Northumbrians are creeping south. He keeps chancing his arm. Our watchmen say he's been poaching in the fens.

RAEDWALD   He won't risk anything against us. We've had too many good harvests. Our men could fight all day.

ACT II

WISTAN   But so far south!

RAEDWALD   Well then! All the more reason not to upset Ethelbert. Her name's Bebbe. She's Christian. Come on! It's time Ragenhere learnt to fight. [*They go.*]

LEOF walks over to TANWEN who is working.

LEOF   Another Christian! What would your mother have said, Tanwen?

TANWEN   Don't ask me, Leof.

LEOF   People look to us.

TANWEN   To you, Leof, not to me.

LEOF   People hear my voice, they listen to my song, but Nia helped them to see. Maybe you can too.

TANWEN   No. I don't have it.

LEOF   Have what?

TANWEN   She never taught me, see, her fever came so quickly.

LEOF   So you know what I'm speaking about?

TANWEN   This is not the right time, Leof.

LEOF   We must stand shoulder to shoulder if we're to defeat these Christians.

TANWEN   I'm not taking anyone's side.

LEOF   Do you want to see them win?

TANWEN   I just want to get on with my life in peace. [*She goes.*]

LEOF stands and watches PUCH giving instruction to SIGEBERT and WISTAN teaching RAGENHERE swordplay.

THE WUFFINGS

SCENE II–2

Shouts off. Around the corner comes the MESSENGER carrying BEBBE. Everyone rushes out to watch.

BEBBE Lift! Lift! Higher! Lift! Stop! Down!

MESSENGER Her Royal Highness, Bebbe, Princess of .....

BEBBE I can speak for myself. I am Princess Bebbe of Kent.

MESSENGER The great King Ethelbert bids me...

BEBBE Yes, yes. You can go now. Go on. Back to your boat!

The MESSENGER goes. BEBBE turns and smiles at the stunned welcoming party.

BEBBE Which one's Wistan?

WISTAN has hidden but EORPWALD drags him out.

WISTAN She's old!

BEBBE Don't worry, boy. You can take your time.

RAEDWALD You are most welcome, Bebbe.

BEBBE King Ethelbert, our glorious High King, sends me to bind our two peoples in our love of Christ.

RAEDWALD How is our ally and my old friend?

A frisky ETHELBERT in night gown chases a young woman (one of the NORNS). He clutches his heart as he catches her, but chuckles as she leads him off.

BEBBE He is well and in good heart.

EDITH [*To herself*] Oh, is he?

RAEDWALD We heard as much and are glad he lives so long!

ACT II

BEBBE   Perhaps the good father here will sing a thanksgiving for our safe arrival...

RAEDWALD   Of course.

BEBBE   ...in the warmth of this great House of the Wuffings.

EDITH   [*Furious*] She can't be serious!

PUCH starts to mumble some prayer as RAEDWALD, PUCH and BEBBE each go down on one knee.

EDITH   Bloody woman. [*Looks for WISTAN*] Wistan, come here!

WISTAN   My Lady?

EDITH   Marry her. Quickly. That's a command.

WISTAN   Why me?

EDITH   You're the best man for the job.

PUCH's prayer blossoms into a Gloria and into a marriage service. WISTAN and BEBBE stand together.

EDITH   [*Whispers.*] Leof! What do we do?

LEOF   Wait, my Lady. There's more news to come I think.

The NORN saunters back to her lair swinging a piece of Ethelbert's attire. The MESSENGER stands mid-doorway.

EDITH   So?

RAEDWALD   Well? Your news?

EDITH   Come on, man.

BEBBE   Tell us, Hredric.

The MESSENGER approaches RAEDWALD.

MESSENGER	The king who has thrice sent me on this long journey from Canterbury to Rendlesham...
RAEDWALD	Yes, yes, Ethelbert.
MESSENGER	...sits at the heavenly feast with Bertha, his queen, in eternal bliss. Long live his son, King Edbald.
EDITH	He's dead then.
RAEDWALD	Long live King Edbald.
EDITH	Then you, my king, are the High-King. [Looks around] Isn't he?
RAEDWALD	Is there any more, messenger?
MESSENGER	King Ethelbert died on the twenty-fourth day of February and the king's council met on the following day. The counsellors acknowledge your claim to be High-King...
LEOF	The sisters weave Raedwald's fate.
BEBBE	Fate moves in the mind of God.
RAEDWALD	The messenger has more to say.
MESSENGER	The counsellors acknowledge your claim to be High-King. But I am told to tell you they cannot accept it...
EDITH	Cannot? Why not?
MESSENGER	...for as long as your people continue to worship Woden and Thunor and Frigg – all your worthless idols.
EDITH	What kind of nonsense is this?
RAEDWALD	Let him have his say. How can we respond if we haven't heard the whole message?
MESSENGER	The counsellors of Kent remind you of your baptism eleven years ago. They do not question your good faith, but they know you returned to your idols, set them up alongside the cross of Christ.

ACT II

EDITH [*Looking at PUCH*] Someone takes notice of you.

PUCH I did warn the king.

EDITH [*To BEBBE.*] You knew this was to be a condition!

BEBBE It was Ethelbert's wish.

EDITH Was it? How do we know? Why does King Edbald not come himself?

RAEDWALD Why should he?

EDITH He is your Under-King. Order him to come and swear what his father said.

RAEDWALD [*To EDITH alone.*] Why does it matter?

EDITH Matter!

RAEDWALD Edith!

EDITH The gods give us our lives.

RAEDWALD You must hide them – your altars.

EDITH You take their side?

RAEDWALD Would you risk my High-Kingship?

EDITH If you reject our gods you risk the wrath of Athelfrith on our northern border?

RAEDWALD Enough! Is this a court where we make decisions by shouting? I have decided. It will be known that Raedwald is High-King. Puch, prepare a service of thanksgiving.

MESSENGER Can I return to my masters with that message?

LEOF Your masters?

MESSENGER King Edbald and his counsellors.

LEOF They are all concerned with this?

RAEDWALD What's your point, Leof?

LEOF It is my ear, my Lord. His words seemed strange. You did not say 'Long live King Edbald and all his counsellors.' Edbald is old enough to rule for himself.

RAEDWALD [*Angry*] This should be a time of celebrations, not of arguments and doubt.

MESSENGER [*Going to leave*] My Lord... [*WISTAN steps in front.*]

RAEDWALD Enough. Raedwald is angry!

RAEDWALD storms off.

LEOF My Lady, Wulfgar has just returned by way of the south coast. He may have something he can tell us.

WISTAN So are we married?

EDITH Yes!

BEBBE Oh boy, don't be so frightened.

EDITH You can start by keeping an eye on your wife.

EDITH and LEOF go. WISTAN stands guard.

SCENE II–3

WULFGAR stands before EDITH and LEOF.

WULFGAR I thought I'd get away from the gossip back here.

LEOF Just tell us the news about Ethelbert's last wife.

WULFGAR That one! She was the Frigg of his life.

LEOF Without the vulgarity, Wulfgar.

ACT II

WULFGAR After forty years of Bertha, his tight-kneed Christian bitch, he was nearly spilling over! This one was a love goddess all right: all potions and love-magic.

EDITH She wasn't Christian then.

WULFGAR I'm not sure she was anything, except a good poke.

LEOF But Ethelbert's court! What do they say?

WULFGAR Most of them turned a blind eye.

EDITH Like our Bebbe.

WULFGAR Old dragonhead? Yes, she held her head up until the boat began to sink. Then she was off like a rat.

LEOF What do you mean, sink? Surely Ethelbert's son, Edbald, was to take over where his father left off?

WULFGAR Oh, yes, including taking over his step-mother.

EDITH [*Laughs*] The young bull!

LEOF Are you sure of this, Wulfgar?

WULFGAR It was common knowledge. They chased each other round the garden!

EDITH Sleeping with his own step-mother! That old trick.

WULFGAR Exactly.

LEOF What about his counsellors?

WULFGAR They bleat, but Edbald's under her spell. And what he's saying is there'll be a good harvest if only people remember the old words, the old ways.

LEOF He has put the Gods back in their right place?

WULFGAR Every one of them. And the likes of Puch tremble in their cells.

THE WUFFINGS

LEOF	This is a wonder.
EDITH	You kept this quiet?
WULFGAR	Taking sides is never good for trade.
EDITH	I'll see you're recompensed.
WULFGAR	No thank you, my Lady. I can't afford to be in debt to anyone.
LEOF	We must tell the king.

SCENE II-4

RAEDWALD returns to find WISTAN with PUCH, BEBBE and the MESSENGER.

RAEDWALD	What are you doing?
WISTAN	The Queen told me to stand guard on ...
RAEDWALD	You take orders from me, do you understand?
WISTAN	Yes, sir.
RAEDWALD	We cannot make enemies of Kent when Athelfrith and his Northumbrians are champing at the bit.
WISTAN	How far south are they now?
RAEDWALD	Athelfrith roams and ravages the west, searching for Edwin, the pretender to his throne.
WISTAN	And what will he say when he hears of your Christian promise to Edbald?
PUCH	Your true allegiance is south, to Kent.
BEBBE	There is much goodwill towards the Angles.
RAEDWALD	Goodwill does not guard our western farmers.

ACT II

BEBBE   But one voice will bind the people, just as weak-mindedness loosens those cords.

RAEDWALD   A wise wife, Wistan. You're more blessed than you think.

Noise outside as EDITH, LEOF and WULFGAR barge in.

EDITH   Trickery! Edbald has turned back to our old gods. His Christian counsellors concocted this plot to turn you against Edbald.

The MESSENGER drops on to his knees for mercy.

PUCH   Raedwald, give all your people a clear sign.

RAEDWALD   You knew of this?

MESSENGER   I was threatened with my life.

EDITH   All three should be banished.

BEBBE   You can't send me back!

PUCH   Wistan has married her.

EDITH   She's as guilty as the rest.

RAEDWALD   Wistan, what do you think?

WISTAN looks between RAEDWALD and BEBBE. BEBBE throws herself at his feet.

WISTAN   Our missionary has room on his back for our friend, hasn't he. After all, he's already journeyed thrice!

RAEDWALD   You wanted a sign, Puch.

They laugh as PUCH is made to carry the MESSENGER on his back. Everyone jeers and cries 'ee-haw' as they are unceremoniously booted out.
The crowd then turns on PUCH's altar and starts blowing out the candles.

THE WUFFINGS

RAEDWALD   Wait! I will not put up with their plotting against me, but I have thrown them out for their sins, not their beliefs. Wulfgar!

WULFGAR approaches with a Standard.

WULFGAR   Kneel to the High-King of Britain.

They all kneel.

RAEDWALD   Let the message go out that I Raedwald, chosen and named by Ethelbert, now swear to guard, support and serve all those who swear loyalty to me, High-King of Britain.

The NORNS approach with SIGEBERT and RAGENHERE.

FATE   Duty will bring choice.

BEING   You have sons.

NECESSITY   You must choose.

FATE   You will rule as High-King.

BEING   You are their father.

NECESSITY   One must be king after you.

RAEDWALD   But which one?

NECESSITY   Under the sun and her light. Under the moon and his light. We spin life-webs. Only we know the fate of men.

ACT III

SCENE III–1

A MAN enters, accompanied by a WOMAN and CHILD. They appear to be a family of artisans. They stand waiting as EDITH enters, followed by RAEDWALD.

EDITH   I said you'd see them.

RAEDWALD Why do they come the back way?

EDITH   They're artisans. The man says they work in gold. And they have something for our eyes only.

RAEDWALD So does every craftsman.

EDITH   His eyes are honest.

MAN   King Raedwald, we are in your debt. We will not waste your time or that of your good Queen.

As he starts to unravel a large bundle, his WIFE stumbles. He takes the CHILD from her. They are clearly all-in.

RAEDWALD How far have you travelled?

MAN   As far as we had to.

EDITH   You're exhausted. I'll get Tanwen.

MAN   No. Let us show you our work first.

The WIFE takes the child again. He starts to unpack the bundle when a loud banging starts. The voice of a NORTHUMBRIAN is heard.

NORTH–1 [*Off*] Open up, bonny lad. There's two hungry men out here.

WISTAN   [*Off*] What do you want?

THE WUFFINGS

NORTH–1　　　[*Off*] To see the King.

WISTAN　　　[*Off*] You do, do you. What for?

RAEDWALD　　Let me get this sorted out.

NORTHUMBRIAN-1 and NORTHUMBRIAN-2, a brawn-and-brains pairing respectively, burst on past WISTAN.

NORTH–1　　　Look, laddy, he'll want to see us when he hears who sent us.

WISTAN　　　Wait a moment. [*WISTAN catches up.*] Sir, it's Athelfrith's men. [*RAEDWALD nods.*] The King will hear your message.

NORTH–1　　　We come to swear loyalty to the High-King.

RAEDWALD　　So Athelfrith cannot come himself?

NORTH–1　　　King Athelfrith sends his highest regard.

RAEDWALD　　What's your message then?

NORTHUMBRIAN-2 takes out and reads a letter.

NORTH–2　　　When Athelfrith brought together the two royal houses of Northumbria, he was opposed by the upstart Edwin. Because of this treachery, Edwin was exiled from Northumbria. It has come to the ears of our Lord that you, King Raedwald, now offer shelter and comfort to Edwin.

RAEDWALD　　Save your breath.

NORTH–1　　　You refuse to hear your loyal subject's suit?

RAEDWALD　　I deny my loyal subject's case. I haven't seen Edwin for twenty years, not since he found a home at Cearl's court in the west.

NORTH–1　　　Cearl is dead.

RAEDWALD　　Dead? Has Athelfrith been to see him then?

ACT III

NORTH–2 So Edwin is on the road again, a wanderer in search of a guardian. My master says his kingdom would be at risk if this bird were allowed to perch here. We've heard he travels with his wife and child.

RAEDWALD We'll whistle if and when we see them.

WISTAN But, sir...

RAEDWALD [*To WISTAN*] Look after them.

WISTAN But aren't we supposed to ...

RAEDWALD They're only donkeys. Just feed and water them before they return.

The NORTHUMBRIANS leave.

WISTAN Sir?

RAEDWALD Let them see how we welcome our guests and report it. Who knows? One day we may be glad of it.

WISTAN goes as RAEDWALD turns back to the FAMILY.

RAEDWALD So now, what have you got to show me?

The MAN unwraps the famous Sutton Hoo stag.

MAN The sign of the hunted.

EDITH My Lord, have you seen workmanship like this before?

RAEDWALD Indeed I have. Some twenty years ago at York when an orphan boy asked me for help. Is he looking at me now, I wonder. Edwin?

The MAN takes off his cloak. It is EDWIN.

EDITH This is Edwin of Northumbria?

EDWIN You see a true man before you now.

THE WUFFINGS

RAEDWALD   This stag, let it become the symbol of our friendship. You are welcome.

EDWIN   You have heard my story from my enemies. Now let me tell you my side.

RAEDWALD   It can wait. Your family needs to rest.

EDITH   [*Calls off*] Tanwen!

EDWIN   But I want to tell it now.

RAEDWALD   Later will do.

WISTAN returns.

WISTAN   My Lord, I have sent men to double our look-out on the bridge.

RAEDWALD   Lucky you escaped Wistan's patrols. [*Turns to WISTAN, confused.*] Stand them down, Wistan. You're too late. [*WISTAN stares at EDWIN.*] And our other visitors – are they satisfied? Wistan!

WISTAN   Gone! They refused fresh horses. They'd barely got up a sweat coming here.

RAEDWALD   They must have a foothold nearby.

EDWIN   Athelfrith's patrols run close to your border. We slipped past them by the Gog Magogs.

RAEDWALD   Then they'll be back, especially now we have this family here.

TANWEN enters.

EDITH   Tanwen, put our guests where Wulfgar beds down.

WIFE   Can my husband sleep on his own? The child has bad dreams.

TANWEN   I can move from my place.

ACT III

EDITH   Very well, Tanwen.

EDWIN   Thank you. You are most kind.

EDITH and TANWEN take the FAMILY off.

WISTAN   Do we want to play host to him?

RAEDWALD   Why not? If Athelfrith wants Edwin so much, he can come here and bark for himself.

The NORTHUMBRIANS and ATHELFRITH, with his banner, enter to watch the proceedings.

NORTH–1   He's there, sir.

ATHELFRITH   Then you'll go back and see them tomorrow, and the next day, and the next day.

NORTH–2   Yes, my Lord.

ATHELFRITH   Athelfrith will not be threatened.

SCENE III-2

EDWIN and EORPWALD are birdwatching.

EORPWALD   Edwin, why do the birds winter here?

EDWIN   They're biding their time before they go on with their journey.

EORPWALD   Tanwen says you're an exile. What does exile mean?

EDWIN   It means you can never fly home. So there, Eorpwald, promise you won't kill any more birds?

EORPWALD   Promise and hope to die. Tanwen says birds tell you your heart.

EDWIN   They do, if you can hear them.

THE WUFFINGS

EORPWALD   Can we come here again?

EDWIN   Of course. Now go and tell your mother what you saw.

EORPWALD runs off. BEBBE watches EDWIN.

BEBBE   All at once Raedwald's court is full of exiles.

EDWIN   You as well? Where do you hail from?

BEBBE   Northumbria. My mother was raised there. She told me stories about the monk who first showed her the true God. His love of birds and animals won her heart and helped her find her faith. Northumbria needs that spirit again. I came here because I thought Raedwald would cling to the Christian raft, but now...

EDWIN   [*Grins*] It's not unusual for marriage partners to look in different directions, is it?

BEBBE   Raedwald's heart is pagan like Edith's, but his head knows the future is with us.

EDWIN   But he kicked out the missionaries.

BEBBE   Rainy days in summer. Jesus offers these people the warmth of hope and the light of life everlasting.

EDWIN   I know your beliefs.

BEBBE   You've said nothing about your own. Who do you pray to?

EDWIN   Whoever my host prays to. An exile has no choice.

BEBBE   This exile keeps faith with her God.

EDWIN   But it's not your choice. It's Raedwald's and I wonder at Raedwald's purpose in it.

BEBBE   He swings around with the wind.

EDWIN   So an exile must be a good weathercock.

ACT III

EORPWALD runs in. EDWIN swirls him around.

EORPWALD   Two men have arrived to talk to my father. They talk about you, Edwin.

EDWIN   What do they say?

EORPWALD   [*Shakes head.*] Wistan told me to get out.

EDITH and TANWEN arrive.

EDWIN   Is my family safe?

EDITH   Safe? Of course they are. Why do you ask?

EDWIN   Nothing.

EDITH   Eorpwald, you must leave Edwin alone.

EDWIN   Alone? No. We have come here to avoid being alone.

EORPWALD   See!

EDWIN   How old is he?

TANWEN   Eleven. [*She pulls a face.*]

EDWIN   Soon be carrying his father's sword then.

EORPWALD   If we had a battle to fight.

BEBBE   Never wish for it. It will happen when it happens.

EDITH   You have a son?

EDWIN   Just a daughter. Born out west.

TANWEN   The west? You come from the west?

BEBBE   Does he behave like it? He's Northumbrian!

EDWIN   My wife is the daughter of Cearl, King of what the Saxons over there call the Welsh. Are you a speaker of

	the tongue? Pwy a'th daniodd di ag anadl y ddraig? [*'Who fired you with the breath of the dragon?'*]
TANWEN	My mother taught me. A dwedodd wrthai am beidio a dangos fy hun. [*'And she told me not to show off'*]. [*EDWIN laughs.*]
BEBBE	Our mothers have a lot to answer for.
EORPWALD	Are they Northumbrians with father?
EDITH	Yes. Athelfrith's men, again. Eorpwald, go and find out what they've come for.

EORPWALD runs off.

EDWIN	Athelfrith's been looting and burning the west. If anyone stands up to him, he shows them the sharp edge of his sword. His men move at night, attack at dawn and bury their dead by noon. Chickens would have more chance with a fox.
BEBBE	Doesn't anyone stand up to him?
EDWIN	There's no talking sense to Athelfrith. In Powys half his force axed to death a whole community of pale-faced monks while the others carefully harvested apples and pears in the Abbey garden. They call him the Twister.

RAEDWALD and WISTAN are seen with the NORTHUMBRIANS. EORPWALD hurries back.

EORPWALD	I can't hear what they're saying, but one of them is carrying a big purse, and took out some gold. Perhaps they want you to make something, Edwin?
EDITH	Did your father take the gold?
EORPWALD	No, they put it away again.
EDWIN	Come here, you rascal. [*EDWIN picks up EORPWALD.*]

ACT III

SCENE III-3

THE NORTHUMBRIANS leave. WISTAN joins RAEDWALD, who watches EDWIN and the WOMEN.

RAEDWALD   Well?

WISTAN   They've doubled the price. If we can hand over his body before morning, they'll triple it.

RAEDWALD   Is he worth it? He's more at home with the women.

WISTAN   He's a troublemaker. I can tell. It's your duty as High-King to stand by Athelfrith. By sheltering Edwin we threaten ourselves.

RAEDWALD   We must ask Leof.

WISTAN   Leof! He's away with the elves these days.

RAEDWALD   You've grown up, Wistan. Would that my sons had your resolve.

WISTAN   Would that I had their father.

RAEDWALD   And you've coined yourself a silver-tongue. That's dangerous.

WISTAN   You have nothing to fear from me, sir. You know I am loyal.

RAEDWALD   I meant dangerous for you.

WISTAN   Me?

RAEDWALD   This is your chance, Wistan, to prove that loyalty.

WISTAN   Sir?

RAEDWALD   Dispose of Edwin! Tonight! I'm giving the task to you. I'm only taking your advice.

RAEDWALD goes. LEOF emerges from the shadows.

THE WUFFINGS

LEOF
Fate often spares the undoomed man, if his courage is good.

WISTAN
You heard what he said?

LEOF
Every blade of grass heard, every stone in the building felt the chill run through your spine.

WISTAN
Must I carry it out? Does he mean, murder him?

LEOF
Next time you'll be wiser with your counsel. A loose tongue is like a bell in the wind. It loses its meaning.

WISTAN
I am loyal to my King.

LEOF
Good. [*WISTAN goes.*] You may mock the darts of the elves, but you'll be on your knees to their masters before the night is out.

EDITH and her party get up to leave as a NORN measures up EDWIN.

EDITH
The air's got chilly. We should go in.

EDWIN
I felt something down my back.

SCENE III–4

During the following the palace is lit up, showing the different rooms. The corridors are marked with candles and the rooms by a bowl and bench. TANWEN fills a bucket outside and goes indoors, putting a bowl of fresh water in each room. EDWIN and his WIFE settle the CHILD.

WIFE
[*Sings.*] My spring-tide! My goldenhair!
My fair-of-face! My high-wind dancer!
Sleep tonight. And sleep.

BEBBE
O Lord of Glory, reveal now your own might through your mysterious skill, and let wall remain upright against wall. This hall needs the care of the Craftsman and the King Himself to repair the house under its roof.

ACT III

EDITH	Tanwen!

WIFE	My lissom sapling! My slow-smiler!
My sun-and-moon! My only daughter!
Sleep tonight. And sleep.

EORPWALD appears and EDITH takes him into RAEDWALD.

EORPWALD	Goodnight, father.

TANWEN appears and takes off EORPWALD. WISTAN sets up an onion on his bench and stabs at it with his dagger. When he succeeds he turns and is sick into the bowl. The CHILD is asleep. EDITH appears and takes EDWIN to the room where he will sleep.

EDITH	Rest well!

As TANWEN returns WISTAN grabs her.

WISTAN	Tanwen!

TANWEN	The boy is in bed.

WISTAN	It's not him I want. It's you.

TANWEN	Don't look at me like that, Wistan. You've got ghosts behind your eyes.

WISTAN	Your mother promised to help if the pain across my eyes ever came back.

TANWEN	Who's been talking to you?

WISTAN	The King commands me.

TANWEN	What have you got to do, Wistan?

WISTAN	Help me, Tanwen.

TANWEN	One moment you're prickly as a hedgehog, the next soft as curds. You make me nervous.

TANWEN runs off and bumps straight into LEOF who clutches her in front of him.

'It's only you can do this'.
Leof (Tom Marshall); and Tanwen (Melanie Barker).

ACT III

TANWEN	Leof!
LEOF	Sshh. Listen to me. It's only you can do this.
TANWEN	I don't want to know, Leof. I told you.
LEOF	It's Wistan.
TANWEN	Let me go then.
LEOF	He's been ordered to kill our guest.
TANWEN	Edwin? No! He can't!
LEOF	Than you must stop him.
TANWEN	Why not you?
LEOF	He's under Raedwald's orders.

WISTAN walks up behind LEOF, who shelters TANWEN so that she hears the exchange.

WISTAN	Leof! Leof! Is that you?
LEOF	What is it, boy?
WISTAN	I need help from one of your wizards, Leof.
LEOF	Down on your knee-bones. Say your prayers.
WISTAN	Which god do I pray to, Leof?
LEOF	What do you want? To do the deed? Not to do the deed?
WISTAN	Do I have a choice?
LEOF	We always have choices, it's whether we have the strength of mind to make them.
WISTAN	I have to do it.
TANWEN	He can't... [*LEOF gags her.*]

THE WUFFINGS

LEOF   Go back to your bed. Wait! [*WISTAN turns and goes.*]

TANWEN   [*Struggles free.*] This is monstrous. [*Rushes off.*]

WULFGAR arrives home. He goes into his room and dumps his stuff. The WIFE screams, waking the CHILD. EDWIN, EDITH, BEBBE and TANWEN come running.

WIFE   Edwin!

EDWIN   What's the matter? Who is he?

WULFGAR   It's only me, Wulfgar.

EDITH   He always does this. Arrives back unexpected.

TANWEN   Let me settle her. [*Puts the CHILD in the cot.*]

BEBBE   Don't worry. We'll get her back to sleep.

WULFGAR   Let me tell her a story.

In the ensuing confusion TANWEN tries to speak to EDWIN, but EDITH takes EDWIN back to his room as BEBBE helps the WIFE and TANWEN settles the child.

EDITH   They'll be fine now.

LEOF approaches as RAEDWALD looks out of his room.

RAEDWALD   I thought I heard something.

LEOF   It's just Wulfgar back again.

RAEDWALD   He does pick his moment!

LEOF   There's still time to call back Wistan.

RAEDWALD   What would it gain us?

LEOF   You know the wise words about guests, how we must honour them. You know how the gods will be angered.

RAEDWALD   Does Wistan have it in him?

ACT III

LEOF Only the sisters know that.

RAEDWALD So the sisters can foretell a deed that will anger the gods?

LEOF Don't try to cheat them. Wistan must be stopped.

RAEDWALD What if the gods allow the deed because our three sisters know it will come to nothing?

LEOF Your mind is knotted. This guessing ill befits a king. You cannot test the gods. Would your Christian friends allow murder like this?

RAEDWALD Their God asked Abraham to sacrifice his son Isaac. That was a test.

LEOF And was this Isaac killed?

RAEDWALD No. He was saved.

LEOF Then Edwin will die. [*He storms out.*]

WULFGAR starts telling a story to the CHILD.

WULFGAR Listen! There was once a wolf called Fenrir. He was the son of a nasty god and a giantess. Now this Fenrir had evil moods and a huge stomach – and that's the worst kind of wolf!

WIFE Don't scare her.

WULFGAR Don't worry. It ends well.

WIFE Go on then.

WULFGAR This wolf, Fenrir, roamed around Asgard, the green-and-gold world of the Gods, and ate everything he could find to eat. He bit and tore and chewed and ate and ate and ate...

EDWIN relaxes in his room. EDITH watches. BEBBE enters, sharpening the friction with EDITH.

BEBBE Wulfgar's turned nightnurse! He loves it!

THE WUFFINGS

EDWIN   She's scared of the night-time, you see.

EDITH   Day never dawns in Wulfgar's stories!

BEBBE   His voice is very gentle. She's taken to it.

EDWIN   A good story will help my wife. It will remind her of home.

EDITH   The place with mountains.

EDWIN   Very cold, very wet and shadows so deep you could fall through them to the bottom of the world.

BEBBE   Poor Edith. Like me, she only knows a land where the wind whistles. There's so much space above us here – no wonder our people worshipped the skygod.

EDITH   Some of us still do. Edwin?

EDWIN   I'm waiting to see.

EDITH   I'll leave you two to get misty-eyed about Northumbria. [*She goes.*]

TANWEN watches as LEOF enters Wistan's room and offers WISTAN a steaming bowl.

LEOF   The gods depend on your success. Now inhale this.

WULFGAR continues his story to the WIFE and CHILD.

WULFGAR   Then the Gods didn't know what to do. Fenrir was so huge and fierce that only the God Tiw dared to feed him. He just lobbed hunks of meat and gristle straight into Fenrir's mouth.

EDITH arrives and listens.

WULFGAR   When Fenrir grew even larger and fiercer the Gods became afraid. So they made an iron chain and said to Fenrir: 'Are you as strong as this?' 'Wrap it round me!' snarled Fenrir. So they did and then Fenrir bunched up

ACT III

all his muscles and he snapped it at his first go. [*The CHILD and WIFE laugh.*]

TANWEN bursts into where EDWIN and BEBBE talk.

TANWEN You must go. We must go. The dark elves are here in this place. My mother was right. Unless we hold on to what we are, we're lost. Mae gelynion o'n cwmpas ymhob man! [*'We are surrounded by enemies'*].

EDWIN Enemies, where?

BEBBE What's she saying?

EDITH steps into the shadows and listens.

TANWEN The King's ordered Wistan to kill you. You must go.

BEBBE Impossible!

TANWEN Leof told me.

EDWIN But the King welcomed us.

BEBBE How can this be?

TANWEN I don't know.

BEBBE If he'll betray you to Athelfrith, he'll betray all of us.

TANWEN We must all go!

EDWIN No! If I go I renounce all right to my kingdom.

BEBBE Your life's in danger!

EDWIN So be it.

BEBBE And your wife and child? Don't they have a right to your life?

EDWIN No man has a right to his own life, let alone another's.

BEBBE What cold reasoning is this?

THE WUFFINGS

EDWIN I can't leave. The king has made me welcome here. If I am fated to die, I'd rather die at Raedwald's hands than at the hands of some lesser man.

TANWEN Well, you can't stop us sitting outside your door.

As WULFGAR continues his story the two women settle down outside EDWIN's door. EDITH retreats.

WULFGAR So the Gods made a chain twice as strong. And Fenrir, he bunched up his muscles again, and shattered it into a thousand pieces. [*They all laugh.*]

RAEDWALD looks out of a window as EDITH enters.

EDITH Are you listening for something?

RAEDWALD Eorpwald says the birds tell you your heart.

EDITH Was it the birds told you to murder your guests!

RAEDWALD [*Sighs*]

EDITH You don't flinch. I name the crime. Murder your own guests. And you toss it away like a forkful of straw. I name it again. Murder your guests!

RAEDWALD Leof says fate will not allow Edwin to die unless the gods will it. Besides Athelfrith is my ally and Edwin's enemy.

EDITH And runs amok in the fens.

RAEDWALD My wife is an army commander now.

EDITH Your wife is the Queen! And you should be the King. The High-King.

RAEDWALD Athelfrith has sworn an oath to me.

EDITH For how long? If he can buy you, he can buy others.

RAEDWALD You want me to break an oath and fight him?

EDITH Set Edwin on his rightful throne.

ACT III

RAEDWALD What! A half-man that runs away to watch birds and gossip with women!

EDITH A man who knows his heart and will be a good leader of his people.

RAEDWALD It would mean defeating Athelfrith.

EDITH Then this land breathes again and thanks Raedwald, High-King of all. From east to west and south to north they say Raedwald is our guardian. He is our leader. There is none like him.

RAEDWALD Then Ragenhere comes with me.

EDITH What?

RAEDWALD If I challenge Athelfrith, Ragenhere rides alongside.

EDITH He's barely sixteen. He's only just started smiling at girls.

RAEDWALD Old enough to flirt, old enough to fight.

EDITH If you can't turn the knife in Edwin, you turn it in me?

RAEDWALD I want to be sure you're interested in the principle, not the man.

EDITH Edwin is honourable. He trusts you.

RAEDWALD He'd still run away if he really knew what's what.

EDITH He does know....and he's already dug in his heels.

RAEDWALD All right. If he's still here in the morning, I will help him win his kingdom.

EDITH Then the Gods will reward you.

EDITH climbs into RAEDWALD's bed. Outside EDWIN's door, BEBBE waits. TANWEN brings some food in a bowl.

TANWEN Do you want to take it in?

THE WUFFINGS

BEBBE
[*Taking the bowl.*] This is a strange partnership.

TANWEN
He spoke to me in my language... the first time someone's done that since my mother died.

BEBBE
Alone! All of us alone in this Anglian wilderness.

WISTAN enters. He is under some drug.

WISTAN
Antan anant anantan. Bright blade, blood blade...

TANWEN
Shh. It's Wistan.

BEBBE
He's drunk!

TANWEN
No, he's crazed. Leof has fired him up with words and weeds! You warn Edwin.

WISTAN sees BEBBE slip into the room.

WISTAN
Slipped into his bed now, has she? Christians! I wouldn't trust them with a potful of piss.

TANWEN
[*Seductively.*] Wistan!

WISTAN
Why are you looking at me like that?

TANWEN
It's the nerve in you. It makes you taller.

WISTAN
Tanwen?

TANWEN
Come here then. [*He backs off*] I thought it was what you always wanted? A Celt saying yes, Wistan, yes.

WISTAN
Tanwen, are you teasing me?

TANWEN
All mouth, am I? Well, come and find out. What are you hanging about for?

TANWEN takes him by the hand and leads him away.

WULFGAR
Now the gods were afraid. They went down into dark caves in the middle-world and asked the dwarves to make a magic fetter in return for a huge hoard of gold.

ACT III

TANWEN lays WISTAN down and dances over him, weaving a kind of spell on him.

WULFGAR The dwarves made a ribbon as smooth as silk. 'Where's the strength in this?' said the Gods, 'What's it made of?' 'Six things,' said the dwarves. 'The sound a cat makes when it moves; a woman's beard; the roots of a mountain; the breath of a fish; a bird's spittle; and the sinews of a bear.'

BEBBE finds TANWEN with an unconscious WISTAN.

BEBBE Tanwen, what have you done?

TANWEN [*Hugging herself.*] Awoken something.

BEBBE Is this pagan magic? Tanwen, have you been using devil's work?

TANWEN You may think so. But it was to save two men.

BEBBE At the price of your own soul.

TANWEN Who cares about that when another's is in danger?

LEOF appears.

LEOF What's happened to Wistan?

TANWEN He's struggling with his demons.

BEBBE Tanwen seems to have some special charms of her own.

LEOF You used them!

TANWEN We must wake him. Help me. Both of you.

BEBBE and LEOF help her drag WISTAN off.

WULFGAR So the Gods showed this smooth ribbon to Fenrir, and he looked at it and snarled, 'Where's the fame in snapping this? Anyone could do it. Unless,' said Fenrir, 'Unless magic has gone into its making, in which case I'm not going near it.'

THE WUFFINGS

EDITH slides away from a sleeping RAEDWALD and approaches EDWIN in his room. She covers his eyes.

EDITH   Ssshh.

EDWIN   Who's there?

EDITH   The one who has shaped your shining fate.

EDWIN   What kind of riddle is that?

EDITH   One who anoints the head of Northumbria's next king.

EDITH bends down and kisses his forehead.

EDWIN   Are you are a sister from beyond this middle-earth?

EDWIN tries to get up.

EDITH   No. You must not see me. Then you don't need to lie to the king.

EDWIN   I expected a noose or a knife, but you?

EDITH   All I ask is a favour in return. One day.

She goes. BEBBE watches her go, then enters.

BEBBE   You cannot leave it any longer.

EDWIN   Now? You said one day. [*EDWIN turns.*] Bebbe!

BEBBE   This house is turning back on itself. It's being tempted by dark forces. Even this stubborn-ness of yours is misunderstood as a stand for the old gods.

EDWIN   I understand your God, Bebbe, but I don't hear him yet.

BEBBE   But you know you will. It is a matter of time. We must not let Him slip beyond our reach. The true God must be the true sword that wins you Northumbria.

EDWIN   What can I do?

ACT III

TANWEN returns.

BEBBE Just do something!

BEBBE leaves him and sits beside TANWEN.

WULFGAR Then one of the Gods stepped forward. 'Fenrir,' he said, 'Let us wind this ribbon round you. And if you can't snap it, we'll set you free. We promise.' 'All right, but I want one of you to put your hand in my mouth as a mark of good faith.' And that, child, is why Tiw has only one hand. But Fenrir the wolf was fettered with the ribbon made by the dwarves – and the gods laughed.

He bends over the child.

There! She's asleep. And safe, from Fenrir. For the moment.

SCENE III–5

Morning. RAEDWALD wakes, gets up, moves past the sleeping bodies and into EDWIN's room.

RAEDWALD He sleeps like his baby.

EDWIN sits up.

RAEDWALD I came to see if your night was a quiet one.

EDWIN Do you look after all your guests with such care?

RAEDWALD I hail your loyalty and your trust. Last night I made a promise... Everyone should hear this.

RAFDWALD picks up the bowl and spoon and bangs on it. BEBBE, TANWEN, EDITH, LEOF, WISTAN, WULFGAR, WIFE all come running.

RAEDWALD This man trusted in the good name of the Wuffings. We owe him loyalty. We owe him friendship. We owe him

THE WUFFINGS

	his homeland. We will march against Athelfrith and show that twister what honour is!
LEOF	The three sisters wove your fate. Woden will bring us victory in this battle. May every man be true to his comrade.
RAEDWALD	Well said, Leof.
EDWIN	My Lord, you asked if my sleep was disturbed.
RAEDWALD	You mean you did have a visitor? [*Smiles.*]
EDWIN	Yes! A vision. Close enough to touch my skin, to whisper in my ear, and anoint my forehead.
RAEDWALD	We've all had those kind of thoughts. [*Laughs.*]
BEBBE	Did this vision say anything?
EDWIN	That if I stayed here and put myself in your hands I should be king of Northumbria.
LEOF	The sisters have spoken to him.
EDWIN	This was no wyrd-speak, my Lord. My guest told me I should be a Christian king.
LEOF	It was just a dream, then.
EDWIN	A spirit that allows me to rise again when I should be dead.
BEBBE	A Christian spirit.
EDWIN	It told me to fight the pagan Athelfrith.
BEBBE	Alleluia.
LEOF	[*To RAEDWALD*] Defeat Athelfrith like that and you serve the Christians!
EDITH	Our army's not going to fight under the banner of Christ!

ACT III

RAEDWALD They are right, we will need the old Gods. Edwin, what sign do we fight under?

EDWIN Whichever will bring us victory.

RAEDWALD Good man. This is a son I could respect. But whatever sign we fight under we lose half our army. So we fight under both. Not as two halves, but as one army under two gods. Where are my sons?

SIGEBERT and RAGENHERE are brought forward.

Sigebert will stay and sing prayers for us. Ragenhere will ride behind me. This way we are double-guarded, double-hardened...

EDITH Double-crossed!

EORPWALD What about me?

SCENE III–6

LEOF In this middle-world the war-eagle flies
And the grey wolf howls, eager for carrion.
Prince and thane, poet and slave:
Each one needs a king he can trust,
Each is glad of treasures in the hall;
And the greatest gift of all is loyalty.

The noise of a blacksmith's forge is heard as hammers ring out. The sounds of bellows, hammers ringing on anvils, stropping of blades on whetstones, clash and clank of armour and weapons, and neighing of horses. The sparks, steam and fire of a forge spills on to the stage. Out of the smoke steps a BLACKSMITH with a red-hot blade which he plunges into water.

BLACKSMITH Skilfully forged in the flame by smiths,
Scarred by chisels, scoured by files...
Harsh is his voice at the head of the host...
Shoots a deadly shaft from his stomach...
Tempered, beaten, stropped, unsheathed...
Hammered, hammered, hammered home.

THE WUFFINGS

The Blacksmith (Alan Edwards).

The WARRIORS walk on, singing a martial song. EORPWALD runs along the line giving each his shield and helping them to prepare. EDITH and BEBBE follow, daubing paint on the warriors' chests. EDITH marks Thor's hammer and BEBBE the extension to make the cross.

The BLACKSMITH lays out on the ground a Christian cross and sets it alight. As they kneel and pray to it, EDITH rushes up and puts sand over the top part to create the hammer of Thor again.

The NORNS approach RAEDWALD.

NECESSITY Son of Woden! Blood of Woden! Raedwald, blood of Woden's blood!

FATE One king makes wise choices and yet suffers grief.
One exile is guest and honours his host.

ACT III

                One boy dies in battle before he can be king.

BEING   Glory for one, sorrow for another.
                    Gifts of the gods, webs of the women.

NECESSITY   You must remember, Raedwald, remember! Honour us.
                    Our ways. Our wyrd. Honour our Gods.

BEING   We who died live in you.

NECESSITY   Look back to look forward.

The WARRIORS rise and prepare for battle.

LEOF   Raedwald the king assembled an army.
                    A thousand Anglians marched north and west
                    Until they reached the banks of the Idle.
                    They hoisted their shields above their heads,
                    And waded through the shining water.
                    So Raedwald and Edwin fought the dragon Athelfrith.

A choreographed battle takes place. The NORNS weave their threads around the individual warriors. ATHELFRITH with dragon standard, is cut down.

LEOF   Raedwald swung Silverfang, his Swedish sword,
                    Which his father owned and Wuffa before him;
                    He shattered the bone-cage of the Northumbrian,
                    He burst open Athelfrith's brain-pan.

RAEDWALD   My friends! My followers! Guardians of the House of Little Wolves! I was fated to win. And I will reward you, one by one. Before he leaves this world, each man must strive to win the praise of all his friends and followers. Edwin!

RAEDWALD stoops to pick up the dragon standard of Athelfrith. He gives it to EDWIN who kneels to accept it. RAEDWALD lays both hands on Edwin's head and raises him up.

RAEDWALD   Edwin! Rise as King of Northumbria!

RAEDWALD beckons EORPWALD and smears blood on his face. He then goes to RAGENHERE and embraces him.

THE WUFFINGS

RAEDWALD   Ragenhere, Eorpwald, you are here! You fought this fight, you see Athelfrith dead. Witness that I, Raedwald, King of the Angles, High-King of Britain, am the man of men and leader of leaders in this island.

As the NORNS sing, the WARRRIORS turn to go.

LEOF   The Wuffing and his warriors gave thanks to Woden.
That hero was High-King of All Britain.
The sun turned red. The moon turned red.
The river Idle oozed away to the sea.

The WARRIORS are silhouetted against a red sun. The sound of a charge and battle cry disperses them all. The NORNS hold up RAGENHERE, and then kill him.

RAEDWALD   My boy! My boy!

Blackout.

END OF THE FIRST HALF

THE SECOND HALF

ACT IV

SCENE IV-1

A weary band struggles on. WISTAN leads with EORPWALD on his back, WULFGAR and WARRIOR carry a stretcher on which lies the body of RAGENHERE. At the back come RAEDWALD and LEOF.

TANWEN, BEBBE and EDITH run out to meet them.

LEOF You must greet the High-King of all land north and south of the Humber!

TANWEN Where's Eorpwald?

WISTAN turns to show EORPWALD on his back.

WISTAN His legs gave out. Cramp!

TANWEN helps EORPWALD down. WULFGAR and WARRIOR lay down the stretcher. EDITH comes over to look.

RAEDWALD He was close by when we stormed their camp. He rode through them like a Rus.

EDITH He rode on his own?

RAEDWALD He escaped my clutches. He was firing their tents and scattering their horses.

LEOF The sword must learn battle.

EDITH Just tell me!

RAEDWALD The battle was over. We thought they'd all fled and turned to tend our wounded. Ragenhere dismounted to help. I saw him bite through one man's webbing and clean his wound with his spittle. But then the best of Athelfrith's men came over the hill opposite. They flew down on us like eagles straight out of the setting sun. Many ran straight on to our spears but the boy's horse had bolted ... and ... and ... he took the man and his horse too. Don't say it. Please, don't say it.

EDITH His gods took him. He had to go.

EDITH drops down to touch RAGENHERE.

RAEDWALD Where's Sigebert?

Silence.

RAEDWALD Where is Sigebert? He must come from his prayers.

BEBBE Sigebert has gone. Fled overseas to the Franks. His Christianity couldn't stomach this. [*Points to pagan emblem.*] He said it was like swallowing his own sick.

EDITH His God took him too.

RAEDWALD Is this my punishment for serving two altars? I have to pay twice? The old gods and the new god gave me victory but each has robbed me of a son.

LEOF No. Sigebert ran away.

RAEDWALD It was his heart too. It made him run like it made Ragenhere fight. He believed he was right. Would we do the same?

LEOF But Ragenhere is dead. We must remember him.

RAEDWALD Yes. Yes! Wulfgar! I want a helmet made. With panels. One shows a warrior kicked down by a horse. But even as he falls he brings down the horse and its rider. Do you hear?

WULFGAR It's not easily done.

RAEDWALD Then go to Sweden for it! They know. Ragenhere fought in the name of his ancestors.

ACT IV

WULFGAR   I'll leave tomorrow.

LEOF   Take him inside. [*RAGENHERE is borne away.*]

RAEDWALD   Add to the helmet a sword and shield. We will have gold buckles and gold clasps inlaid with garnets. We will wear treasure!

LEOF   Glory to Raedwald!

RAEDWALD   We will drink, we will sing! We will have a palace of peace, and gather together a treasure-hoard as rich as the hoard buried with Beowulf. I am Raedwald. I am High-King. I will rise in splendour! I will ride high and bright as the sun! You see, Raedwald can choose when the time is right.

EDITH   And Sigebert?

RAEDWALD   Who?

EDITH looks aghast at him as he goes. TANWEN leads off EORPWALD.

EDITH   Tanwen.

TANWEN   Shall I put him to bed?

EDITH   Yes. Then come to me.

SCENE IV–2

WULFGAR sings a shanty, which intersperses with the time-shift.

WULFGAR   Sting of the salt! Rip of the wind!
    Hurl-and-clap-and-boom of the sea!
    Sting of the salt! Rip of the wind!
    Landlubber, will you come with me?
    Now down the whale's way,
    Gull's path and seal's bath,
    Down to the whale's way.

THE WUFFINGS

'Sting of the salt! Rip of the wind!'
Wulfgar (William Haden).

ACT IV

> Leap of the heart! Race of the blood!
> Chuck-and-sip-and-sob of the sea!
> Leap of the heart! Race of the blood!
> Landlubber, will you come with me?
> Now down the whale's way,
> Gull's path and seal's bath,
> Down to the whale's way.

The celebration continues into a formal dance that gradually turns into a time shift.

LEOF   In the first year following the battle with Athelfrith, we made our flat cakes once again in the month of the returning sun.

TANWEN and EORPWALD dance together. WISTAN watches.

WISTAN   He doesn't hold you right.

TANWEN   He's no clumsier than most men.

WISTAN   Let me show you.

TANWEN   No, Wistan, your wife wouldn't like it.

LEOF   In the second year the winds blew again during Hretha's month.

RAEDWALD and EDITH dance by.

RAEDWALD   We haven't danced for years.

EDITH   And everyone's looking. I hate it. What are you all looking at?

LEOF   In the third year the winds were still blowing in Eostre's month.

WISTAN and BEBBE dance by.

BEBBE   You don't have to hold me so far away.

WISTAN   I don't have to dance with you at all.

BEBBE   Then don't!

THE WUFFINGS

LEOF In the fourth year, cows were milked three times a day in the month of three milkings.

BEBBE and WULFGAR dance by.

BEBBE I didn't know you could dance.

WULFGAR There's lots of things you don't know about me.

BEBBE That's because you're never here.

LEOF In the fifth year Wulfgar sailed north during the first travelling month.

WULFGAR Ireland ahoy! Iceland ahoy!
Geysir, glacier, lava and scree!
Ireland ahoy! Iceland ahoy!
Landlubber, will you come with me?
Now down to the whale's way,
Dolphin dance! Sea-steed prance!
Down to the whale's way.

TANWEN and EDITH dance by.

EDITH When are you going to take me, Tanwen? The weather's good.

TANWEN I don't know.

EDITH Leof says you know the magic.

TANWEN You musn't tell anyone.

LEOF In the sixth year during the second travelling month the sun shone all day.

TANWEN and WISTAN dance by.

WISTAN Are you showing the Queen your secrets?

TANWEN No.

WISTAN You are. People have seen you.

ACT IV

TANWEN — You can't threaten me, Wistan. Eorpwald will look after me.

LEOF — In the seventh year, one more grew up.

EORPWALD replaces YOUNG EORPWALD and dances with TANWEN.

LEOF — The month of weeds was rife with tares, for it was silver-gold with barley.

TANWEN — Stop holding me so close.

EORPWALD — I like holding you close.

TANWEN — You're not a little boy any more.

EORPWALD — That's how you taught me.

TANWEN — I'll tell Leof.

WULFGAR — Home sails the heart.
And home sails the man.
Back from the whale's way,
Back from the deep sigh,
Home sails the heart.

LEOF — In the eighth year the first full moon of winter forecast a cold season.

EDITH and RAEDWALD dance by. RAEDWALD stumbles.

EDITH — What's the matter?

RAEDWALD — I don't feel so good.

RAEDWALD is seized by a fit of coughing and has to be helped off.

LEOF — In the ninth year the blood month was marked by strange happenings. Orange lights in the shaking sky.

TANWEN and EDITH dance by.

EDITH	Nine sticks from nine branches from nine trees and Woden hung on the tree for nine nights. A time of wonders.
TANWEN	I cannot alter these things. You know that.
EDITH	We'll meet tomorrow, at the same tree.
LEOF	In the tenth year the Yule was red and green and frost-bitten and Wulfgar turned for home.
WULFGAR	Sting of the salt! Rip of the wind! Hurl-and-clap-and-boom of the sea! Sting of the salt! Rip of the wind! Landlubber, will you come with me? Now down the whale's way, Gull's path and seal's bath, Down to the whale's way.

SCENE IV-3

TANWEN and LEOF, now with stick, are in the midst of plants by the pool, searching.

TANWEN	...take the female hop-plant, wormwood, betony, lupin, vervain, henbane, dittander, viper's bugloss, bilberry plants,...
LEOF	Come on! Remember!
TANWEN	Stop getting angry.
LEOF	Then listen to what I say! The queen won't like your carelessness. You meet tonight. Cropleek..
TANWEN	Cropleek, garlic, madder grains, corncockle. Lift the whole plant, never damage the roots. Commit to the plant with your blood.

TRAVELLERS appear. They are EDWIN, PUCH, ETHELBURH.

TANWEN	Who are they?

ACT IV

LEOF Don't you recognise him? With his new bride!

TANWEN It's King Edwin of Northumbria. What happened to his wife then, the Welshwoman?

LEOF She died with their last child.

TANWEN [*Cradles plant.*] Never damage the roots. Commit to the plant with your blood.

EORPWALD jumps on TANWEN. He does not see LEOF.

EORPWALD Hey, sorceress, will you put a spell on me?

LEOF Eorpwald? What are you doing out here?

TANWEN and EORPWALD look sheepish.

EORPWALD I, er ...

LEOF The King's son?

TANWEN You won't tell anyone!

LEOF shakes his head and goes.

TANWEN You must watch out, Eorpwald, for my sake.

EORPWALD Where do we go? That copse again?

TANWEN I can't. I've got to see your mother.

He follows her off.

SCENE IV–4

A banging on the door. WISTAN, BEBBE, RAEDWALD and EDITH hurry on to stand in front of the entrance.

EDITH Why do they have to come in person? What's wrong with a messenger?

RAEDWALD Edwin is always welcome in my palace.

THE WUFFINGS

EDITH   So long as he doesn't bring any more Christian visions.

RAEDWALD   Ten years on and he's still sitting on the fence.

EDITH   He only has one vision now. Your High-King's crown!

An exchange of looks. Another bang on the door.

EDITH   And he still likes to make a good entrance.

RAEDWALD nods to WISTAN who opens the door. EDWIN steps forward. Beside him is ETHELBURH, a vision of hair. Concealed behind both is PUCH.

EDWIN   Ten years since I stood on this threshold. But this time no disguise.

EDITH   This time a new woman, if I'm not mistaken.

EDWIN   Ethelburh.

EDITH   Ethelburh?

EDWIN   Daughter of your old friend, King Ethelbert of Kent.

EDITH   Ethelbert!

ETHELBURH   My mother, Queen Bertha, often spoke of you.

EDITH   That makes her sister of Edbald, the boy who ...

RAEDWALD   Edith!

EDITH   ... so loved his step-mother.

EDWIN   The Queen is teasing you.

BEBBE   Ethelburh, you are known to me and very dear.

ETHELBURH   Thank you, kind Bebbe. [*They embrace.*]

EDITH   Christians! They cling together like bats.

EDWIN   [*To ETHELBURH.*] You see? Just as I promised.

ACT IV

RAEDWALD   What brings the king of Northumbria all this way east?

EDWIN   I come straight from Kent: to renew my oath of loyalty and ask your blessing on our betrothal.

EDITH   Is that all?

Behind EDWIN, PUCH coughs.

ETHELBURH   You know our companion, I think.

PUCH takes off his cowl.

EDITH   How dare you bring him back here?

EDWIN   I ask your indulgence, Raedwald, to allow this man back through your kingdom.

ETHELBURH   He is my confessor. He exchanges letters with the Holy Father himself.

EDITH   That donkey cuts no ice here.

ETHELBURH   I only ask that the Bishop may cross...

EDITH   Bishop!

RAEDWALD   Bishops in Kent, are there? This is news. We thought the bishops left long ago.

PUCH   They did, but have now been replaced. King Edbald was baptised not six months ago.

RAEDWALD   Baptised? He walked into the sea?

ETHELBURH   Why should he do that?

PUCH   You did not have to walk in like that.

RAEDWALD   When I did that I wanted to be High-King. [*To ETHELBURH.*] Is that what your brother is after?

ETHELBURH   My brother, High-King?

83

THE WUFFINGS

EDITH	And a man who climbs into the bed of his father's bride. The church accepts that too?
RAEDWALD	It seems it cannot afford not to.
PUCH	The church accepts Edbald as a committed Christian, who dutifully agrees to convert his people.
EDITH	Again?
RAEDWALD	[*Turns to EDWIN*] And you? You were invited to this ... bath-time?

EDWIN looks embarrassed.

EDITH	What are these snakes up to?
EDWIN	My Lord, there is no plot.
RAEDWALD	Not as you see it.
PUCH	With respect, it was at the request of our Holy Father, like this marriage.
ETHELBURH	He wrote to us both.
EDITH	[*To EDWIN.*] The Holy Father wrote to you?
RAEDWALD	The King of Northumbria has chosen to follow Christ?
EDWIN	When I am ready I will do it because it is true.
BEBBE	A safe answer.
PUCH	But you will be baptised if you are to marry my charge. The Holy Father has told Ethelburh it is a condition.
EDWIN	As I have said I would.
PUCH	Do it for your love of Christ alone.
BEBBE	And Christ's love of his fellow man. His love begins and ends with that hope or it is nothing.

ACT IV

EDWIN   Bebbe is right. As King, I have to act for my people, not my God.

PUCH   But when those people are misled? What counsel do we seek, but God's own divine purpose?

ETHELBURH   Why does the Holy Father not write to Raedwald and his wife?

PUCH   He did once.

RAEDWALD storms off.

WISTAN   They're all mocking us. [*To EDWIN.*] I should have killed you when I had the chance.

EDITH   Wistan! Follow the King and make sure he comes to no harm. [*WISTAN goes.*] You'll be eating and sleeping here, I suppose. That's going to be fun. I hope Leof's got one of his monster stories.

TANWEN appears. EDITH goes to her.

TANWEN   Oh, sorry! [*To EDITH*] Will we still go?

EDITH   Why not?

TANWEN   You have visitors. I thought you might not want to.

EDITH   Of course I do.

As TANWEN waits, BEBBE corrals EDWIN, PUCH and ETHELBURH.

ETHELBURH   Who's that?

BEBBE   She's the one who put the spell on my husband. Sees things. Heals sores, warts and the like.

PUCH   Tanwen, a sorceress?

ETHELBURH   What do you mean?

EDWIN   I understood she saved my life.

WISTAN returns to whisper in EDITH's ear.

EDWIN	The king is not well?
EDITH	You want to be measured for his mantle now?
WISTAN	I'll measure him like the fates did ten years ago.
EDWIN	You mistake our purpose in coming.
EDITH	I thought you had no purpose. You fooled me last time. It won't work again.

EORPWALD runs on.

EORPWALD	Mother, please come. Father is coughing up blood.

They all go off, leaving only PUCH and TANWEN.

SCENE IV–5

PUCH watches TANWEN. LEOF appears behind.

LEOF	Like bees' wax, isn't it?
PUCH	What?
LEOF	Temptation. Once it softens, your whole church slithers and slides in on itself.
PUCH	I know what temptation is.
LEOF	Yes, there's so much suffering in your creed.
PUCH	Your gods, Woden, Tiw, are the cause of suffering. Our God suffered for us.
LEOF	And spread around guilt like dung. You Christians, you're all wading in it. What we have done, what we have not done!
PUCH	Hope! Love! Atonement!

ACT IV

LEOF   Retribution, that's the old way, and it's the best way.

PUCH   You're a limpet, Leof. Stranded when the tide went out.

LEOF   Lord of men, save me from this arrogant fool.

PUCH   We'll soon see where the people's hearts lie.

LEOF   The battle is fought and won, Puch. When the wind clears the mist, we'll see who the victor is.

PUCH   Leof, the days of your nine sticks are gone. Your last one barely props you up. [*PUCH kicks away LEOF's stick and he falls.*]

    WISTAN enters.

WISTAN   Leof!

PUCH   He fell. [*Goes.*]

WISTAN   [*Helping up LEOF*] The king is very ill.

LEOF   We'll need all our wits now to keep these ravens at bay. They can smell death. Eorpwald may be our only chance. Where is he? Where's Tanwen?

SCENE IV–6

    EDWIN enters with EORPWALD.

EDWIN   It had wings the size of a crow but this strange colour on its head.

EORPWALD   I said I'd be back soon. My father needs looking after the whole time.

EDWIN   It was a kind of red, very vivid.

EORPWALD   A small patch on the back of its head?

EDWIN   I think so, yes.

EORPWALD   A black woodpecker. We hardly ever see one.

EDWIN   It was over there. I hadn't seen it before either.

EORPWALD   They don't fly across here very often, although they breed just over the sea.

EDWIN   [*Glances up*] Here's where I saw it. [*They stare up into the tree.*] Can you see anything?

EORPWALD   No.

EDWIN   We'll give it a moment and see if it comes back.

EDWIN sits down.

EDWIN   Who looks after the king? Your mother?

EORPWALD   She just tires him out. Leof tells us what to do, and Wistan watches over him.

EDWIN   You know what must happen when your father does die?

EORPWALD   Whoever my father chooses becomes High-King.

EDWIN   Not quite. Whoever all the other kings think right and swear oaths to. Without that, the name of the High-King is hollow. It means nothing.

EORPWALD   Then why do you need my father's blessing?

EDWIN   Because his word counts for so much. Eorpwald, I know he's ill, but he must choose. If he dies without picking one of us, if it's not clear who will be High-King, we will have squabbles and skirmishes and small wars.

BEBBE and PUCH arrive.

EORPWALD   What do you want me to do?

EDWIN   Call Wistan away. We must speak to Raedwald alone.

EORPWALD   My mother would never agree to it.

ACT IV

BEBBE   Eorpwald, you are old enough now to make your own choices. You will be the next king.

EORPWALD   Not if Sigebert returns.

PUCH   If only.

BEBBE   It's not likely. He prefers the kingdom of God.

EDWIN   So we will be kings together, Eorpwald. We must learn to work together. The old world is dying. Friendship is the finest armour.

PUCH   Our Holy Father says .....

EDWIN   There it is! [*Pointing into the pool.*]

EORPWALD   Where?

EDWIN   [*Looks up to the sky.*] There! Follow it, Eorpwald. The bird shows you your path, your heart!

EORPWALD follows it.

EDWIN   You must bide your time, brother Puch. When we see Raedwald, don't push him into choosing me. Don't corner him. He must choose the king, not the god.

PUCH   But you're here, Edbald isn't. He knows you've won.

EDWIN   Why?

PUCH   Because of the damned pagan beliefs you're holding on to. I presume that's why you're doing it.

EDWIN   You don't know what Raedwald's beliefs are.

PUCH   They were imprinted on my backside when I was expelled.

EDWIN   That was just saving face. Wouldn't you say, Bebbe?

BEBBE   He's never had to make up his mind. He's always let Edith do it for him.

EDWIN   Yes, so we must speak to him without Edith.

SCENE IV–7

RAEDWALD is brought on. He lies on a bed and is being massaged by TANWEN, who sings as she works. EDITH watches her intently. RAEDWALD groans and turns.

EDITH   He's like an old pig, snuffling and rooting around for the last acorn.

WISTAN enters.

WISTAN   Leof said the king was not to be disturbed.

EDITH   He won't be if you keep your voice down. She's very gentle.

WISTAN   Then why do it?

EDITH   Your tireless loyalty to the King is not in question, Wistan. Where are our visitors? What are they doing?

WISTAN   The woman brushes her hair.

EDITH   And the others?

WISTAN   Talking as usual. In very low voices.

TANWEN   Why don't they move on?

WISTAN   They want to wait until he's better.

EDITH   No, Wistan. They're waiting for him to die!

RAEDWALD   [*Turns over.*] Either way, they'll have a long wait.

EDITH   That's the spirit! Hang on for Eorpwald!

RAEDWALD   Eorpwald! High-King?

EDITH   Why not?

ACT IV

WISTAN	He should not be tired like this.
RAEDWALD	You value it too highly. High-King! What have I gained? Nothing but isolation.
EDITH	We have lived! We have made laws, settled disputes, held the peace, worshipped the great gods...
RAEDWALD	Who they all abandon: Sigebert, Edbald, Edwin soon.
EDITH	So choose Eorpwald.
RAEDWALD	He commands no respect. Better now, I think, just to hand over to Edwin.
EDITH	Reward Edwin? After he betrayed both of us?
RAEDWALD	He betrayed you?
EDITH	Calling me a Christian spirit. I saved his life!
RAEDWALD	Who betrayed whom on that night, Edith? Did you betray me? With Edwin?
EDITH	How did this idea get inside you?
RAEDWALD	It crept into my head like everything else. Guard it as I die, Edith.
EDITH	You've got plenty of life left in you.
RAEDWALD	Let me be spared thoughts.
WISTAN	You must go, dear Queen. He must rest.
EDITH	Tanwen!

TANWEN follows EDITH out.

SCENE IV–8

TANWEN and EDITH are in a wood. TANWEN absorbs the sounds of the wood. EDITH follows and obeys.

EDITH   Where are we going?

TANWEN   Stop. Sit down here. [*EDITH sits.*]

LEOF hurries in and looks at TANWEN.

LEOF   He's not with you? Where is he then?

TANWEN   I don't know.

LEOF goes.

EDITH   Who's he talking about?

TANWEN   Eorpwald. Come. [*They continue.*] Close your eyes. What do you see?

EDITH   Nothing.

TANWEN   Good. Now open your heart. Don't tell me. Feel.

EDITH   How can I take in everything?

TANWEN   Bit by bit. Remember how the Goddess Frigg had to find every plant in order to protect the innocent one from harm. Imagine! You go from flower to flower; each herb, each grass, each moss.

EDITH carries on looking. TANWEN follows.

SCENE IV–9

WISTAN stands guard over RAEDWALD. EORPWALD arrives to watch, but stands back as LEOF comes through.

RAEDWALD   You have served me well, Wistan.

WISTAN   And will always do so.

RAEDWALD   I am drowning, Wistan. I am lost. Like the swimmer who heads for the shore and then turns back. This way, that way, this way, no... I am lost. The tides will take me. Which God will save me?

ACT IV

LEOF   I thought you prayed to both.

RAEDWALD   Leof! It's twenty years since I was given the sign of the cross by the old Saint with black eyes. I have watched some accept this new God, others resist him. I have followed every twist and turn, and I still don't know!

LEOF   Your heart, listen to your heart.

RAEDWALD   I don't know my heart! All I hear are words, arguments. So much icy reason, so much fiery passion, and each gives the lie to the other. Pagan values, Christian values, and the outcome is I don't believe in either.

WISTAN   You're wrong, my Lord. You are still captain of the ship.

LEOF   Where's Eorpwald? Tanwen doesn't know.

RAEDWALD   But the ship's capsizing. Can't you see? And the rope from the shore...! The rope! No ... No!

LEOF   Guard him. Let no one near.

The NORNS weave their webs and sing.

FATE   You will die.

BEING   You are High-King.

NECESSITY   So you must choose.

RAEDWALD   How can I choose for everyone?

FATE   A king has to make choices.

BEING   It is time to choose, Raedwald.

NECESSITY   You must choose wisely.

RAEDWALD   My fate, my word, my duty. How can I know?

EORPWALD rushes in.

EORPWALD   What's the matter?

THE WUFFINGS

WISTAN	His mind... it's spinning.
EORPWALD	You must go and get the Queen.
WISTAN	She's with Tanwen. I don't know where they go.
EORPWALD	Then find Leof. He knows.
WISTAN	He's looking for you.
RAEDWALD	[*Screams.*] Get out of my head!
EORPWALD	Then tell him I'm here with my father. Go on. Quickly! He's dying, Wistan.
WISTAN	I said I'd stay here with the King.
EORPWALD	You'll trust him with his own son, I hope?

WISTAN leaves, reluctantly. EORPWALD sits by his father's head and calms him.

EORPWALD	Father.
RAEDWALD	Is my son my friend?
EORPWALD	Yes, father. I think he is.
RAEDWALD	You have been out with Edwin?
EORPWALD	To watch birds.
RAEDWALD	What do they say?
EORPWALD	Say?
RAEDWALD	The birds tell you your heart, remember? What do they tell you?
EORPWALD	They tell me their lives are short. Edwin told me a story. We're in the hall one winter night, a starless night with the wind blowing in off the sea, when a sparrow flies in. It flickers round and round in the warmth, in the firelight. It hears the laughter, the songs, the old stories. Then it

ACT IV

flies out and away into the dark again. The lives of pagans are like this, Edwin says, like this sparrow. Just a little bright time in this world before we go back into the cold and the darkness. So if this new teaching can offer us anything, any knowledge and warm hope about what happens after our lives, we should accept it.

RAEDWALD   You will be Christian?

EORPWALD   When the time is right, I think I will.

WISTAN finds EDITH and TANWEN.

WISTAN   Come quickly. The king is dying.

EDITH and TANWEN rush off with him.

SCENE IV–10

EORPWALD beckons PUCH, EDWIN and BEBBE to stand around RAEDWALD's bed.

RAEDWALD   You stand before me like the three sisters.

EDWIN   High King, we are here only to learn our destiny.

RAEDWALD   I knew you had come... knew you were waiting for something.

EDWIN   We wait only for your word.

RAEDWALD   My word! Since when have you waited for that? You decided to marry Ethelburh. It's the Pope's word you wait on now.

EDWIN   We need to know who will be the next High-King. My father-in-law, Ethelbert, named you as his successor eleven years before he died.

RAEDWALD   Eleven years, yes. My guts remember the wait!

EDWIN   We are willing to wait as long.

THE WUFFINGS

RAEDWALD   We?

EDWIN   Edbald of Kent and I.

RAEDWALD   It was my baptism that pleased your father-in-law, Edwin.

EDWIN   So I have heard.

RAEDWALD   So I should choose Edbald. He's been baptised.

EDWIN   It's my loyalty to you caused me to wait.

RAEDWALD   Which horse to jump on? Always a vexing decision. The quick one for the short charge or the sturdy one for the long escape.

EDWIN   And King Raedwald knows that choice well.

RAEDWALD's laugh turns into a coughing fit.

RAEDWALD   But you've forgotten another candidate.

EDWIN   The West and South Saxons are at each other's throats and the East Saxons still squabble over their land. Who else is there?

RAEDWALD   You forget my son, Eorpwald.

BEBBE   But he is not King. Whoever is High-King must first be a king.

RAEDWALD   Who says? [*To PUCH*] Him?

PUCH   Nothing is written down, but no man can be High-King without the support of all the other kings.

RAEDWALD   I thought this tribal jostling was a thing of the past. I thought Christians believed a son rightfully inherits from his father.

PUCH   You wish to confess your sins?

EDWIN   On his death bed?

ACT IV

PUCH — It's never too late.

EDWIN — His people wouldn't understand.

RAEDWALD — Edwin will join me perhaps?

EDWIN — I will need to talk to my counsellors.

BEBBE — Why do you do this? This base trading in front of your own son.

EORPWALD — I understand my father's wishes. He seeks what is best for our people.

RAEDWALD tries to sit up, coughs and collapses.

BEBBE — Edith should be here.

PUCH — You know what is best for your people.

RAEDWALD — But for Athelfrith we would have had peace for half a lifetime. Why not leave well alone?

PUCH — And leave your people to darkness and damnation?

RAEDWALD — Whatever I choose, it will only lead to more suffering.

BEBBE — He should not be tortured like this.

RAEDWALD — And the truth is there is no choice. Edbald, Edwin eventually, and you Eorpwald. The three of you! Three in one, one in three. [*Laughs.*] You're all the same. [*He makes the sign of the cross.*]

BEBBE — I will go and get Edith. [*She goes.*]

PUCH — The truth is often bitter.

RAEDWALD — It's not you who has to swallow it.

PUCH — Our Lord died for it.

EDWIN — It's not that easy, Puch. There is so much to weigh up. From day to day.

THE WUFFINGS

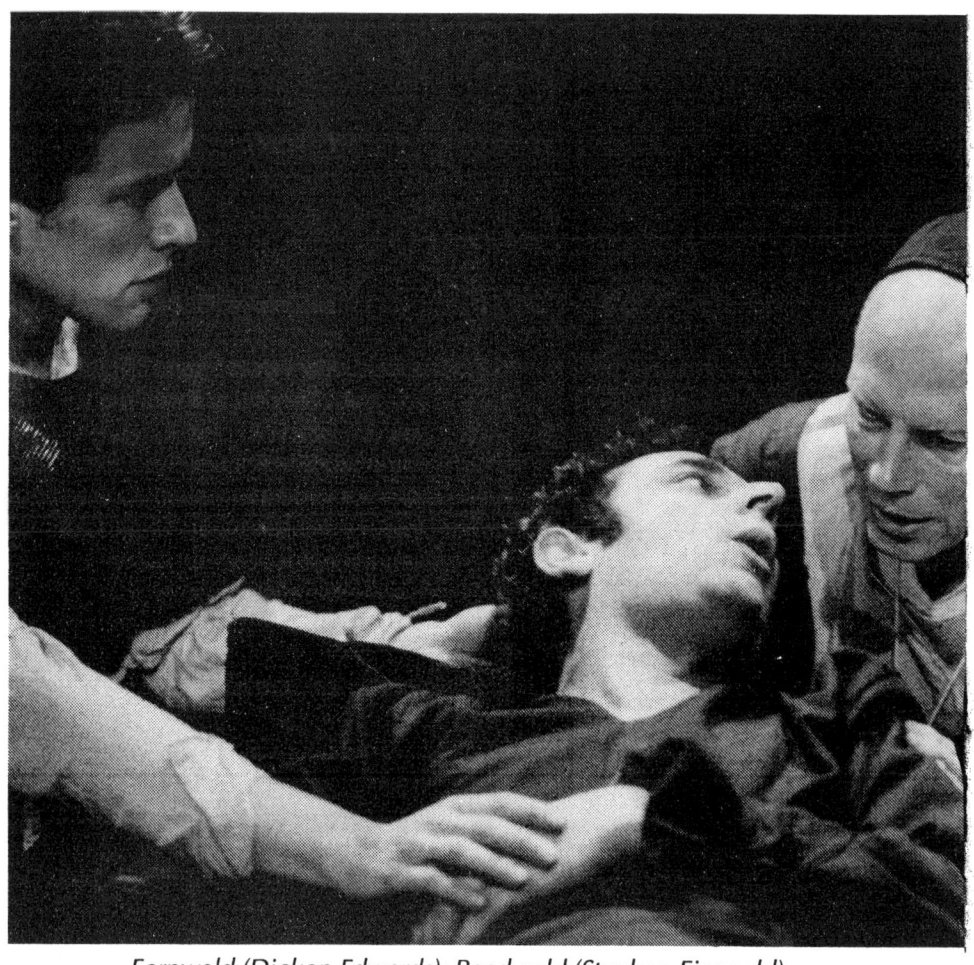

Eorpwald (Dickon Edwards); Raedwald (Stephen Finegold); and Puch (Alastair Cording).

PUCH   You cannot bargain with God.

EDWIN   Each of us must find his faith according to his own thoughts, her own feelings.

PUCH   Not if you want your wife!

EDWIN   You threaten me?

EORPWALD   Listen. He does not breathe.

    EORPWALD closes RAEDWALD's eyes.

ACT IV

PUCH   You know what we must do.

EDITH, BEBBE, WISTAN, LEOF and TANWEN tumble in.

EDITH   What are you doing here?

PUCH   He asked for us. Did he not?

EORPWALD   Yes, mother, he did.

She sees RAEDWALD.

BEBBE   [*To EDITH*] He smiled ... he was peaceful.

PUCH   His last wish was to be accepted into God's good grace.

EDITH   What?

PUCH   He is with the angels.

EDITH   [*Screams.*] No! [*She is restrained by BEBBE and EORPWALD.*]

WISTAN   [*Drawing his sword.*] You liar!

EDWIN   [*Drawing his sword.*] I was here. I heard his words. So did Eorpwald.

EORPWALD throws himself crying on RAEDWALD.

EORPWALD   Father!

EDWIN   Long live the King!

ACT V

SCENE V–1

The body of RAEDWALD is laid out.

LEOF [*Sings*] When? How? We cannot say.
All we know is we must die.
Old age, illness or sword's edge.
We must leave this shining world,
And we must strive before we die.
Old age, illness or sword's edge.
The praise of those surviving us
Is living fame when we die.
Old age, illness or sword's edge.

EDITH I should have been at his side.

LEOF You couldn't have saved him.

EDITH I could have stopped those ravens stealing his soul.

WISTAN enters.

WISTAN Your son wants to see you.

EDITH He can wait. If he chooses to befriend them, he can't expect his mother's love.

WISTAN He's the King now.

EDITH Not until his counsellors say as much. Until then he's plain Eorpwald.

LEOF [*Going.*] Perhaps I should see him.

EDITH No, Leof, I want to talk to you. Wistan, Tanwen, please leave us on our own.

WISTAN and TANWEN go.

ACT V

LEOF   Lady?

EDITH   This is no good. We all keep bluffing to avoid the trial of strength.

LEOF   What do you propose to do?

EDITH   I am going to visit the other world.

LEOF   The other world? You?

EDITH   Tanwen told me I could.

LEOF   She's wrong. Leaving this world is only for the shaman and the few with starcraft.

EDITH   You mean men?

LEOF   No! Some Celtic women say they can do it.

EDITH   Like Tanwen's mother, Nia.

LEOF   She claimed so.

EDITH   And Tanwen too. She has the gift. She would come with me.

LEOF   Out of the question. You can only travel alone.

EDITH   So it is possible.

LEOF   You don't know the dangers you might face.

EDITH   Tanwen will tell me.

LEOF   But you're in mourning.

EDITH   All the more reason. My six senses are tuned like harpstrings.

LEOF   You must be careful, Edith. Prepare the way. You must not lose your mind.

EDITH   My mind is made up. I want to be sure that Raedwald's spirit is safe within their web. If not I want to know. I'm not allowing these Christian soul-thieves to steal his name.

LEOF   And if his spirit isn't there?

EDITH   Do you want them to get away with it?

BEBBE enters.

BEBBE   Lady! If there is anything I can do to help with your husband's funeral?

EDITH   Probably, when we know what form it's going to take.

BEBBE   What form?

EDITH   Yes. Who knows what we're going to do with him?

WULFGAR enters.

EDITH   Wulfgar!

WULFGAR   What a time to return. [*They embrace.*]

BEBBE   Is she mad?

LEOF   Not by my measure.

WULFGAR   I always seem to arrive in the thick of it.

SCENE V–2

We hear steps and singing. Light cascades through a door as EDITH descends into the arena. It is HER vision.

TANWEN   [*Off*] What do you see?

EDITH   Bleakness, blackness. Wait! I can hear the sound of water.

TANWEN   You must let go of me. I can come no further.

EDITH   Wait!

ACT V

TANWEN   Trust in yourself.

EDITH   I can't see a thing! Tanwen! Tanwen!

The light slowly increases casting an eerie glow across the terrain and revealing the tree and well. The sound of water increases. EDITH descends and walks towards the NORNS who splash water from the pool on the tree.

WODEN in a blue broad-rimmed hat comes on, carrying a spear and wearing an eye-patch. As he approaches her he raises his spear.

EDITH   All-Father!

WODEN   My daughter.

EDITH   My Father.

WODEN   All that you know I know. All that the gods know I know.

EDITH   And the sisters?

WODEN   You know them already. Fate, and Being, and Necessity.

The NORNS look up as their names are called.

                    Your world is their web until the nine worlds drown.

EDITH   [*To NORNS.*] Will you tell me, is Raedwald here?

WODEN   They cannot answer such questions.

EDITH   But I have to know.

WODEN   Three in one and one in three.

FATE   Your fate is to die.

BEING   Your being is the Queen.

NECESSITY   Your necessity is to bury your husband.

EDITH   I know these three things.

THE WUFFINGS

WODEN   Then what else is there to know?

EDITH   How shall I bury him, and where, and when?

WODEN   None of these things can be known.

EDITH   Allfather! Why?

WODEN   You live on middle-earth, you cannot pay the price. [*Points to his eyepatch.*] See! I paid the price of this eye to drink from that well and learn wisdom. I am the keeper of the mead of poetry.

A vision of WODEN hanging crucified on the tree.

                      I hung from that windswept tree. I hung there for nine long nights. I was pierced with a spear. I was an offering to Woden, myself to myself. I peered at the worlds below. I seized the runes of wisdom. Shrieking I seized them. Then I fell back.

A WOMAN goes to the well in a shawl and pulls up water which she splashes on her belly. She is pregnant. When she turns we see it is TANWEN.

TANWEN   [*Sings*] I have never seen those shapes,
                      I have never climbed those hills;
                      But I will know them when I see them,
                      I will call them mother-home.

EDITH   Tanwen? [*TANWEN does not hear her.*]

TANWEN   They are waiting away west
                      – Strength to my heart, strength to my feet! –
                      And I will know them when I see them,
                      And I will call them father-home.

EDITH   The water blesses you!

TANWEN   This is the song White Fire sings,
                      This is the beat her wild heart beats.
                      Cantuc, blue and rising
                      – Hills unchained, home of the free.

ACT V

TANWEN goes.

EDITH   That is your journey, Tanwen. But where is my husband? Is he here?

WODEN   No one can know these things unless they surrender themselves.

EDITH   But I will give anything. I must find out.

WODEN   You cannot. You are human. You must trust in yourself. That is your great power.

EDITH   Is Raedwald there? Is he with you?

She turns to the NORNS once again.

EDITH   Sisters of wyrd, tell me the threads of my husband. Where is his fate?

FATE   Raedwald's fate was to leave the earth at his appointed hour.

EDITH   But where is he now?

BEING   Raedwald is on his last journey.

EDITH   But which way is he going?

NECESSITY   Raedwald must be given the means of his journey.

EDITH   Yes. Of course. Yes! We give him the means. We enable him, we choose which way he sails on his last journey. [*The vision begins to fade.*] Yes!

TANWEN   Lady!

EDITH   Yes!

TANWEN   Lady!

EDITH   Yes!

THE WUFFINGS

SCENE V-3

WISTAN runs in. We are back in the hall. He helps TANWEN sit EDITH up. EDITH looks up at everybody.

WISTAN	What have you been doing, Tanwen? Is this your magic?
EDITH	A boat!
TANWEN	A boat?
EDITH	He travels by boat. I want a boat. I've decided. We're going to bury him in a boat. If he's not there, we'll send him there. His last journey.
WISTAN	She's not well. Fetch Leof.
EDITH	I'm right as rainfall.
WISTAN	A boat?
EDITH	Get Wulfgar. He'll know. Wulfgar!

WISTAN hurries off.

EDITH	You never told me about the child.
TANWEN	You saw that too?
EDITH	You were at the well. Whose is it?
TANWEN	I cannot tell you.
EDITH	You can't or you won't?

WULFGAR arrives, followed by WISTAN and LEOF.

EDITH	Shall we start again? I want a boat.
WULFGAR	A boat?
EDITH	Yes, a boat. This is becoming tedious. You know what a boat is, don't you?

ACT V

WISTAN How big?

EDITH How big have you got?

WISTAN The ferry?

EDITH No! As big as we put to sea in.

WISTAN Who?

EDITH Raedwald. My husband. Wulfgar! You know what I'm talking about.

WULFGAR I think so. You want a ship burial.

WISTAN You want to bury him at sea?

EDITH No, to be buried in the earth. A ship-barrow, like Beowulf's in the poem.

WISTAN All the boats are in use.

EDITH Then have one made.

WISTAN There's no sawn wood.

EDITH Tear it off the churches then.

WULFGAR There is the boat we keep up the creek.

EDITH There you are.

WULFGAR But it's ninety feet long.

EDITH All the better.

WULFGAR Do you know how long that is?

EDITH [*Pointing.*] From there... to there. I'm not an idiot, Wulfgar.

WISTAN But to get that on to land.

EDITH Not just on to land. Up on to the Hoo.

THE WUFFINGS

WISTAN   Up the cliff? It can't be done!

EDITH   Can't! I have just pushed my wits to the edge of the world for you and your kin, you small-minded little runt. Can't! Never use that word in front of me again.

WISTAN   No, my lady.

WULFGAR   We use rollers and ropes, and huge teams of people. I've seen it done in the north. Scaled, oiled and waxed, then cradle the ship in earth.

EDITH   You'd better arrange the boat then, Wulfgar. Wistan, you get the weapons and armour together. Tanwen, find his eating bowls. I will clothe him. The House of Little Wolves is ready to hear its history. Leof must make his poem shine. This burial will set Asgard alight and show the people that Raedwald lights a sky-path for them.

SCENE V-4

BEBBE pursues PUCH.

BEBBE   Has Edith any grounds for this abomination? Did Raedwald confess his sins?

PUCH   You doubt my word? You doubt Edwin?

BEBBE   I doubt two men with so much to gain from it.

PUCH   I must advise Eorpwald – about this shameful funeral.

BEBBE   If you hadn't tried to rub their noses in it...

BEBBE watches him go as WISTAN finds her.

WISTAN   The Queen wishes you to lay out the King.

BEBBE   Me? I'm not having anything to do with this wicked burial.

WISTAN   You are my wife. You'll do as you're told.

ACT V

WISTAN hits her and BEBBE falls to the floor. He is about to hit her again just as WULFGAR enters.

WULFGAR No! Your queen would be disgusted at you.

WISTAN goes. WULFGAR helps BEBBE up.

BEBBE You see what this has done? It divides us all.

WULFGAR He caught the sharp end of the Queen's tongue.

BEBBE He's been sour for longer than that. His mouth is stuffed full of sloes.

WULFGAR So try to understand.

BEBBE She wants me to prepare the body!

WULFGAR Why not?

BEBBE For this pagan...

WULFGAR Just do it.

BEBBE We should all be pulling together.

WULFGAR You wait until you see the boat. We'll all be pulling together then.

BEBBE Sometimes I think you've no scruples at all.

WULFGAR I can't afford them, nor fences or land-markers. I'm on no one's side. That's best for trade.

BEBBE, shocked, turns to go as EDWIN walks on.

BEBBE Your scheming has caused all this. Do you know where it will end?

EDWIN I think so, yes.

BEBBE One day you'll trip over your own shadow.

BEBBE goes.

THE WUFFINGS

WULFGAR — I told her, she gets too worked up. The old dog must have his last bark.

EDWIN — Do you want a hand?

WULFGAR — Is the King of Northumbria offering to pull?

EDWIN — Death is a great leveller. Edith's set on it.

WULFGAR — Edith to you, is it? You're as sly as they say you are. You can lead one of the rope-teams. Wistan's leading the other. We start at first light.

WULFGAR goes as EORPWALD and PUCH enter.

EORPWALD — I can't stay away. He was my father. Tell him, Edwin.

PUCH — This is sheer heathenism.

EDWIN — Compromise, brother, remember?

PUCH — He weakens his new authority.

EORPWALD — I weaken that if I don't attend.

EDWIN — Isn't there something personal you could lay down? Something he really cared for: a wishbone, a harpstring? Not some pagan relic but something personal.

PUCH — [*Laughs.*] Yes, yes, of course. Go and tell your mother you'll be there. I'll meet you later.

EORPWALD — And you'll think about the other thing?

PUCH — I'll try.

EORPWALD goes.

EDWIN — What other thing?

PUCH — He's got some girl pregnant.

EDWIN — And you give him advice?

ACT V

PUCH   As to his Christian duty. [*PUCH goes.*]

EDWIN   Perhaps we should just find her. It shouldn't take long.

In another place EORPWALD and TANWEN are seen.

TANWEN   You will be king.

EORPWALD   If my brother stays away.

TANWEN   They say you will be Christian anyway.

EORPWALD   Perhaps. Tanwen, I've asked for help for you.

TANWEN   You've told them! You shouldn't have done that!

TANWEN goes, EORPWALD follows. EDWIN watches as EDITH and LEOF enter.

EDITH   The son attends his father's funeral. I suppose we should be satisfied.

LEOF   It's like shouting into a gale. You hear yourself and think you're roaring, but those who need to hear you only see an empty mouth.

EDITH   If that's all you can offer you might as well jump in beside him, Leof.

EDWIN   Raedwald was a great king. The first to bring together all the kingdoms into one. Who knows if we'll see his like again? It is right to do him honour in this way.

EDITH   I suppose you want me to thank you.

EDWIN   It's Eorpwald you should thank. Make peace with your son. He will need you to guide him and guard him.

LEOF   We thought he sought that from you.

EDWIN   I can't give it. His real danger is on his own doorstep.

WISTAN marches up to EDWIN.

THE WUFFINGS

WISTAN   Wulfgar says you head the other rope-team.

EDWIN   Is that all right?

WISTAN   No. North or south team?

EDWIN   I'd better take the north.

WISTAN goes.

EDWIN   Eorpwald needs friends he can trust.

LEOF   Raedwald never wanted for support.

EDWIN   I don't doubt it, but wise support?

EDITH   We can look after our own and will make sure the name of Raedwald is remembered.

EDWIN   You think a poem and a pile of earth will be enough?

LEOF   It's a story that will be handed down.

In the distance PUCH enters carrying a small bundle. He waves it at EDWIN and smiles as he passes by.

EDWIN   Our grandsons and great-grandsons will be the judges of that.

EDWIN goes off after PUCH. BEBBE arrives.

BEBBE   My Lady, if you still wish me to make your husband ready.

EDITH   Thank you, Bebbe. Thank you. [To LEOF.] Play him out, Leof. Praise him with words that people will recall and repeat. Tough words that withstand the winds of time.

EDITH goes with BEBBE. LEOF is left in the centre, an old man with a stick. He summons up his last breath.

SCENE V–5

LEOF   The King is dead! Cry for Raedwald!

ACT V

> Cry him to Woden's hall on high
> Where each day the heroes fight,
> And fell each other, heal and feast,
> And wait for the time at time's end
> When gods and heroes wrestle with giants;
> When hot stars whirl down from heaven
> And black earth sinks into the sea.
>
> Raedwald! Raedwald! Raedwald! Raedwald!

EDWIN and WISTAN haul ropes as they encourage their men. WULFGAR stands at their head and manages them.

WULFGAR   Heave! Heave! Heave! Heave! Slow down on the left. You're skewing it!

WULFGAR goes up to WISTAN.

WULFGAR   It's not a tug-of-war. You must pull together. Now!

They start pulling again.

WULFGAR   Keep up on the right.

A cry, further down, stops them.

VOICE   Man under! Man under!

WULFGAR   Stop! Stop!

WULFGAR rushes down to help.

EDWIN   What's eating you, Wistan?

WISTAN   You're two-faced.

EDWIN   We're all two-faced. It's what gives us our sense of balance.

WISTAN   You mock what we do. Mock the men who sailed in this boat.

WULFGAR   Leave him! We can't let it sink into the mud.

THE WUFFINGS

EDWIN   Ever feel you're at your own funeral, Wistan? Digging your own grave? Run with the tide. It's the first rule of sailing.

WISTAN   I sailed in this boat under men who would have eaten you for breakfast.

EDWIN   True enough, but their only loyalty was to the man at the helm, the god with one eye. But he's overboard, isn't he, drowned in the new current. Your boat's powerless.

WULFGAR   That was nasty! But there it is, it's sorted out! Are we ready? One, two, three! Heave!

WISTAN   The only power outside the boat is from the wind and the moon. Your God offers nothing.

EDWIN   My God. Not yet.

WISTAN   As good as.

WULFGAR   Come on. We've barely got her arse out of the water. Heave!

The NORNS sing as everyone processes on with flaming torches, chanting. Gradually the shape of a longboat is made out as WULFGAR stands over a central chamber.

WULFGAR   I name the whetstone.

ALL   Sign of the King!

WULFGAR   I name the banner-stand.

ALL   Sign of the High-King!

WULFGAR   I name the sword.

ALL   Sign of the warrior!

WULFGAR   I name the shield.

ALL   Shield of his people!

WULFGAR   I name the helmet.

ACT V

ALL Guardian of thoughts.

WULFGAR I name the cauldron.

ALL Sign of the old ones. Sign of Sweden.

WULFGAR I name the stag.

ALL The stag of friendship.

WULFGAR I name the buckle.

ALL The sign of justice!

WULFGAR I name the coins.

ALL Sign of the giver!

WULFGAR I name the harp.

ALL The harp of story!

WULFGAR I name the lamp.

ALL The lamp of journey!

WULFGAR I name the horns.

ALL Heard through the nine worlds!

WULFGAR I name the fire.

ALL Fire of the Gods!

A fire is lit on the silver dish.

WULFGAR Asgard swallows the smoke! Let the dead man live!

ALL Let him live! Let him live! Let him live!

As the fire dies down, WULFGAR beckons to EORPWALD to climb on to the top of the burial chamber.

WULFGAR Your gift.

THE WUFFINGS

EORPWALD reaches inside his cloak and produces the pair of spoons given by Augustine. He raises one spoon in each hand to show them off.

EDITH   No! No! [*LEOF holds her.*] He can't. He can't do it.

WULFGAR   We said something for his journey.

EORPWALD   You said something personal.

EDITH   Wulfgar! [*Rounds on WISTAN.*] You, Wistan. Stop him! What are you made of?

WISTAN looks round for more support but everyone is frozen.

                 Tanwen! [*TANWEN does not move.*] You slut! You Welsh slut!

EDITH turns to EDWIN. They meet each other's gaze and stand their ground until EDITH backs off.

BEBBE   [*Sinking to her knees*] In nomine patris et filii et spiritu sancti.

EDITH   How dare you?

BEBBE   [*Ignoring her.*] Amen! Amen! Amen!

EDITH   Stop that woman!

EORPWALD   Except a man be born of water and the ghost, he cannot step into the Kingdom of God. [*Turns to the coffin.*] Father, your spoons: Saul and Paul, the great enemy of Christ who became the great friend of Christ. I name the spoons.

BEBBE   Sign of Christ.

EORPWALD   [*Looking for a response.*] I name the spoons!

ALL   [*Except for EDITH*] Sign of Christ.

EORPWALD lays the spoons beside the coffin and climbs out with WULFGAR, who closes the chamber, leaving the lamp burning.

ACT V

They all circle the ship, except for TANWEN who slips away.

EDITH   Tanwen! Where is she? Tanwen!

TANWEN is disappearing west.

TANWEN   Whatever comes of it, I have chosen. Home of the free. Home of the free. For my mother, for myself, for the child inside me.

TANWEN disappears. The flaming torches are extinguished.

LEOF   A great gathering: countless people.
The Anglians feared the sky-signs
And feared the darkness of days to come.
They feared their enemies, they feared themselves.

               After Raedwald, Edwin became High-King of Britain. But he was baptised and so betrayed the Gods.

               Edith, the old queen, lost her senses. She talked to herself, whistled to the birds.

               And Eorpwald the Unlucky, son of Raedwald, ruled the Anglians for only four years before the traitor Wistan stabbed him in the neck. Wistan was done to death, his body bound and thrown overboard off Dunwich.

               The people begged Sigebert to sail home from Gaul, but he was king for less long than Eorpwald. He went into battle brandishing a wooden cross, and was put to the sword.

               Listen! House of the Little Wolves
Is the song of yesterday, seed of tomorrow.
What mind-tides! Heart-winds!
All this, and still the poet sings.

THE END

'A great gathering: countless people'.

Eorpwald (Dickon Edwards), Bebbe (Janet Jefferies) and Attendant (Katherine Oliver) at the play's conclusion.

THE WUFFINGS

PRODUCTION NOTES

This is a play about choices and anyone thinking of producing it must make up his or her own mind about design, music, costume etc. Much will depend on the intended style of production, cast size, and resources available. Nevertheless there are things we discovered in the first production that might make some of those choices easier:

SETTING/SITE
The epic nature of the play demands a special kind of performance space. Eastern Angles' original production took place in a converted agricultural warehouse on a stage 30m wide; as wide as the original Sutton Hoo boat was long. It is not necessary to repeat this, but you do need some way of combining a space for spectacle with the means of keeping the audience close to the action.

STAGING
The play is epic in style, so changes of locations must be quick and easy and the action allowed to become seamless in its progression, even allowing scenes to overlap each other. Too much furniture or scenery will be an obstacle to this. You must have a selection of entrances and exits that allows actors to get on and off stage without crashing in to each other and to reach the centre of the stage quickly.

DESIGN
Quite apart from the staging demands described above, naturalistic settings will be impossible. Certainly, you should not attempt to bring a boat on to stage! We used a set of beautifully-made benches to suggest boats, funeral pyres, portals, even timber-framed buildings. Whatever props you use must be real objects, and justify their own existence before you use them metaphorically.

The most obvious difficulty is the treasure itself. Since it is priceless and incomparable, you will be on a losing wicket from the start if you try to emulate it on stage. As with all the above, you have to find a metaphor for the essence of the thing. In our case it was a large reflecting curved brass (but to look bronze) wall, which stood majestically centre stage and summed up the wealth of this dynasty and some essence of its culture. It also allowed us to conceal central entrances and keep various props close to the stage centre.

Similarly, in costume terms we never aimed to compete with the re-enactment societies. We could not afford the wardrobe bills, let alone the armourers' bill or the jewellers'. Since the show must find its own unity, its own style, this governs all the use of jewellery, weapons, footwear as

PRODUCTION NOTES

well as props. We used simple metal rods for weapons, twisted metal for jewellery and tough men's boots for footwear. To help tell the story, which is fairly complex, we opted for simple black for pagans and white for Christians.

However, it should not be forgotten that this era was one of great colour. Forget the sackcloth and ashes images! The Anglo-Saxons used dyes and were expert at weaving cloth. Moreover they travelled far and wide and picked up influences from all over Europe and beyond.

THE ELEMENTS

We believed that an important way of establishing the feel of the period was to accentuate the elements. Earth, air, fire and water all had a special role in our production. The acting area was created with ten tons of sand tipped over a base of turf. This prevented the sand moving too much and worked as insulation against the hard concrete underneath. Within this area were embedded large open tanks of water. The water could be used for washing, splashing, cooling the blacksmith's sword (when carbon dioxide was bubbled through it), and, with light, to reflect on the brass wall. Over the top of the central area were hung nine bowls as if in mid-air. They too caught the light and the waters' ripples. Finally, we placed an upturned drum by the Norns's area and piped a gas supply to it to create a permanent fire throughout the show. All other fire could then be lit from it. We also had a sunken pit for a hearth fire during the Beowulf scene, candles, burning bowls for pagan ceremonies, a burning cross in the pre-battle build up, and the final image of flaming torches for the creation of the buried ship. This use of flame and water was vital in helping establish the elemental nature of life at this time.

Safety note: any use of fire must only be contemplated in full discussion with your local Fire Officer. For example we were only allowed the brazier effect because there was sufficient ventilation, the gas bottle was situated outside the building and the brazier had a tap close to the drum itself. Similarly, all other fire effects were capable of being doused at a second's notice – the sand and water were handy in this respect!

MUSIC

Music must be integral to the show, although the play is not intended as a musical. Rather, the music is crucial in helping to convey the sense of otherness of the age and to help us understand the characters' relationship with their gods.

Music is also one of the most useful dramatic tools. It allows you to highlight, to background, to colour and to celebrate. You can make time pass, speed-up or stop. It labels characters and un-labels them, it sets scenes and finishes scenes, it relaxes and tightens moments. In short it is

THE WUFFINGS

probably the single most important thing after the text and actors in determining the meaning the production will convey.

For example, in our production we highlighted the boat motif at the end of the Beowulf section (Act I, sc. 6) with a dirge, backgrounded all of Raedwald's indecision with the Norns' wailings, coloured the everyday business during the time-changes and celebrated Raedwald's crowning as High-King. We made Nia first fierce and fundamentalist when she burnt offerings to the gods, then human in the boat as she sang to the wives. Tanwen inherited her gift. In the long conspiracy scene (Act III sc. 4) when Edwin is nearly murdered, music suggested a relaxed night-time, then heightened the sense of doom as Wistan went beserk.

There is much scope for chants, hymns, dirges and traditional songs. We used amalgams of Anglo-Saxon, Old Norse and Icelandic words to settings provided by our musical director, Pat Whymark. At first we were unsure in what direction to look for the forms of music to use. The Wuffings claimed Swedish ancestry but Scandinavian folk song is by and large fairly recent in origin. Most medieval music is Christian and the earliest dates from some 400 years after 625 AD. Eventually, we turned to the music of one of the Finnish nomadic tribes, the Sami, who had moved north to escape the so-called civilising of the mainland. In particular we listened to the singer Mari Boine, who, with her use of yodel and soaring vocals seemed to embody the spirit of pagan celebration and worship.

LIGHTING

This play offers wonderful opportunities for lighting: racing clouds, thunderstorms, smoky halls, shadowy corridors, battles, funerals, descents into the lower world and the final ship burial all offer exciting scope for spine-tingling effects and spectacle. Restraint should be paramount. In fact we turned the lights out during the final ship burial in order to let the simple flicker of hand-held torches have their effect.

Ivan Cutting
Director of **The Wuffings**

PRODUCTION NOTES

RECOMMENDED READING

Bates, Brian, *The Wisdom of the Wyrd* (London, 1996). Very 'new age', but fascinating look at the workings of the *wyrd* pysche.

Branston, Brian, *The Lost Gods of England* (London, 1957). The best introduction to the pagan gods as they existed in pre-Viking Britain.

Campbell, James (ed.), *The Anglo-Saxons* (Oxford: Phaidon, 1982). A good general introduction to the subject.

Carver, Martin, *Sutton Hoo – Burial Ground of Kings* (London: British Museum Press, 1998). The most recent update from the highly readable and pungent Director of the Sutton Hoo Research Trust.

Crossley-Holland, Kevin (ed. and trans.), *The Anglo-Saxon World* (Oxford, 1982). The texts of poems and prose which illustrate the characteristics and attitudes of the age.

Crossley-Holland, Kevin (trans.) and O'Donaghue, Heather (ed.), *Beowulf* (Oxford 1999). The finest literary work to have survived from Anglo-Saxon times, and one of the world's great epic poems.

Evans, Angela, *The Sutton Hoo Ship Burial* (London: British Museum, 1986). The standard museum guide to the subject with good illustrations of the treasure and its location.

Higham, N. J., *An English Empire* (Manchester, 1995). A new and radical reading of Bede that throws much light on Raedwald's place in history.

THE WUFFINGS

CHRONOLOGY

364 AD	Saxon seafarers begin to molest the southern shore of England.
383	Many Roman troops leave Britain. Three subsequent withdrawals leave the country exposed to Picts and Scots, and to Germanic tribesmen.
410	Romano-Britons are cut off from Roman imperial government and left to fend for themselves.
446	British leader (maybe Vortigern) invites a Saxon leader (maybe Hengest) and his warriors into Britain as mercenaries. More tribesman from north-west Europe soon arrive and settle in England: Jutes in Kent, Saxons in southern East Anglia and the Home Counties, and Angles in the east and north. The native Britons (Celts or Romano-British) are enslaved or move west.
c.550–70	The first Wuffing King, Wuffa, rules the East Angles.
c.580	Ethelbert of Kent becomes only the third High-King of the southern kingdoms. He is married to Bertha, a Frankish princess and Christian.
597	Augustine lands on Thanet island with 40 missionaries. Ethelbert, fearing the use of spells, refuses to meet him except under an open sky.
c.605	**Raedwald, King of the East Angles, is baptised in Kent.**
616	**Ethelbert dies and Raedwald becomes High-King.**
617	**Raedwald defeats King Athelfrith of Northumbria by the River Idle, just south of Doncaster, to put Edwin on the throne.**
c.625	**Raedwald dies and is buried at Sutton Hoo.**
	Edwin becomes next High-King and two years later is baptised.

PRODUCTION NOTES

627	Eorpwald is killed by the pagan Ricbert. Sigebert is brought back from Gaul but gives up the crown for a monk's cowl.
c.635	Penda of Mercia crosses the newly erected embankment now known as Devil's Dyke and invades East Anglia. Sigebert is dragged out of his monastery but will only go into battle with a stick. He is killed.
664	Synod of Whitby, when the English church turned Roman rather than Celtic. It effectively marked the conversion of the Anglo-Saxons to Christianity.

GLOSSARY

AEGIR	A god of the sea. He had a hall under the waves.
ASGARD	The world of the gods.
BEOWULF	The hero of the Anglo-Saxon epic poem known by the same name. As a young man, he kills two monsters; he becomes King of Geatland (south of Sweden) and, in old age, kills and is killed by a dragon.
EOSTRA	A spring-like goddess who has given her name to the Christian festival of Easter.
FATES	The three demi-goddesses of destiny, known as Fate, Being and Necessity. They sit under the world ash, Yggdrasill, and weave the lives of human beings.
FENRIR	A huge wolf, one of three offspring of the trickster Loki. He is bound by the gods and will remain so until the end of the world.
FREYR	The god of sunshine, rain and fruitfulness.
FREYJA	The goddess of sexual love and marriage.
FRIGG	A fertility goddess, and foremost of the goddesses. She was the wife of Woden and mother of Balder.
GEATS	The people of Geatland in the south of Sweden.
GOG MAGOGS	The low hills near Cambridge which together with the Fens and Devil's Dyke came to symbolise the boundary of the East Anglian region.

THE WUFFINGS

GRENDEL
: The monster who terrorised the Danish Court. Beowulf wrestled with him and ripped off his arm.

IDUN
: The goddess of youth. She is guardian of the golden apples which are eaten by the gods each day.

THUNOR
: The second of the gods after Woden, who was his father. He was god of war, thunder (caused by the wheels of his chariot as it rolls across Asgard), and of law and order.

TIW
: A god of war, and the bravest of the gods. By sacrificing one hand, he enables the gods to bind the wolf Fenrir.

WODEN
: Foremost of the gods. He is the fearsome god of inspiration (in poetry, in battle), wisdom, magic and death. He won wisdom by sacrificing one eye to drink from the well of Mimir, and by hanging himself on Yggdrasill, the cosmic ash tree.